Presented To:

From:

Date:

MOMENTUM

MOMENTUM

WHAT GOD STARTS NEVER ENDS

ERIC JOHNSON & BILL JOHNSON

DESTINY IMAGE® PUBLISHERS, INC.

P.O. Box 310, Shippensburg, PA 17257-0310

"Promoting Inspired Lives"

This book and all other Destiny Image, Revival Press, MercyPlace, Fresh Bread, Destiny Image Fiction, and Treasure House books are available at Christian bookstores and distributors worldwide.

For a U.S. bookstore nearest you, call 1-800-722-6774.

For more information on foreign distributors, call 717-532-3040.

Reach us on the Internet: www.destinyimage.com.

ISBN 13 TP: 978-0-7684-3992-2

ISBN 13 Ebook: 978-0-7684-8924-8

For Worldwide Distribution, Printed in the U.S.A.

1 2 3 4 5 6 7 8 9 10 11 / 13 12 11

DEDICATION

I dedicate this book to my Dad and Mom for their relentless pursuit of God's goodness and for making sure the nations of the world experience it as well. Thanks for helping to cultivate in me a heart to be a worshiper. Your lives have taught me so much about inheritance and living in the abundance of the King.

To my wife, Candace. You are my lover and best friend. God was having a good day when He created you. Thanks for demonstrating how to live and love life so well. I am having the time of my life with you and so look forward to growing old with you.

To my children, Kennedy and Selah. The day you were both born is a day I will never, ever forget. The both of you are an absolute blessing to your mom and me. You bring such pure joy and excitement to our lives. Thanks for making us so proud.

To my Grandparents. This book is here largely because of the lives you have chosen to live. Thank you for letting us stand on your ceiling. You are my heroes!

To the generations of people whom I will never see. This book is for you to get a glimpse of your revival history and the ground that we paid a price for. Now it's your turn to run into the things God has for you.

ACKNOWLEDGMENTS

A special thanks to Josh Larson and Pam Spinosi for your time and energy in helping to edit the manuscript for this book. I owe you big time. This would not have been possible without you.

Also, thanks to Don Milam for allowing so much grace and stretching the deadlines. Thanks a bunch.

Also, a special thanks to Phillip Breja, Elana Marlo, Samuel Diener, Christina Chadney, and Anette Rodahl. Your research and your transcription of my messages helped to get this thing started. Thanks!

ENDORSEMENTS

Momentum is a remarkable book that has captured the core values of the Kingdom of God. It shows us how to live in full confidence as sons and daughters and yet remain poor in spirit, fully dependent and trusting, like a little child.

It teaches us how to abide in the unshakable security of the Father's embrace. When we know the ceaseless, bottomless, unending love of God that drives out all fear, we become unmovable in the face of all that stands in opposition to God's goodness.

The truths contained within this book will help position a generation of laid-down lovers to receive the greatest inheritance imaginable and to empower them to bring transformation to the world around us.

The Johnsons have taught us more about Christian family than words could ever express. It is an honor and privilege to call them friends.

HEIDI BAKER, PHD
Founding Director, Iris Ministries

Spiritual inheritance is an imperative truth to be recaptured by the Body of Christ. Through *Momentum,* the Johnson lineage continues to unwrap this gift of spiritual inheritance, bringing the wonder and mystery of inheritance back into the forefront of our understanding.

BOB HARTLEY
Deeper Water Ministries

Eric Johnson has written one of the most important books for this hour. We live in an unprecedented time in church history when revival is sweeping across the nations. Yet in the midst of this outpouring, there is a longing to see the current move of God not end with this generation but continue for generations to come. I have given my life to see a generation in revival, and the truth and revelation found in *Momentum* is critical for revival. Inheritance and connection between the generations are among the most misunderstood and mishandled subjects in the Body of Christ, but ones we must understand clearly to move forward. Eric has brilliantly and precisely dealt with the issue of inheritance in *Momentum.* He writes not from a place of theory but from a deep place of wisdom and grace that he lives out every day. Young and old need to read this book.

BANNING LIEBSCHER
Jesus Culture
Author of *Jesus Culture*

Many believers have forfeited the blessings and benefits that are theirs as sons by not having a father's blessing. Heaven on earth is a family business! The foundation of spiritual inheritance in the Kingdom of God is the relationship of a father to a son and vice versa. The momentum of living from inheritance and not toward inheritance is the impartation of this book. Bill and Eric Johnson have given my life a new momentum.

Leif Hetland
President—Global Mission Awareness

This book is a living demonstration of Malachi 4:5-6. As Bill and Eric unite, as father and son, in the compilation of *Momentum,* the convergence of generations is exemplified and thus, a unique depth of revelation is unearthed. I believe a legacy will be left in your heart as you discover your personal spiritual inheritance as a child of God and are raised up to stand on the shoulders of your forefathers. I highly recommend this outstanding book.

Ché Ahn
Senior Pastor, HROCK Church
President, Harvest International Ministry
International Chancellor, Wagner Leadership Institute

From a rich spiritual heritage, Eric shares his heart and what he has learned through the years of living in this environment. He shares how, although many have never had this heritage, it is open to all. In *Momentum,* he clearly tells us that this Kingdom of richness is our inheritance and something for us all to step into and stand in who we are. The life stories that are shared in *Momentum* will impact us all. Along with his dad, Bill, Eric will help us all see what is rightly ours in this amazing Kingdom that we are invited to share in. Good job, son. You hit the mark!

Beni Johnson
Author of *The Happy Intercessor*
*(and mother to Eric)

Eric Johnson is emerging amidst a rich spiritual heritage. Instead of being intimidated by this heritage, he is allowing it to carry him forward. That is the main point of his first book, *Momentum*. How can we be propelled forward by our spiritual inheritance rather than being swallowed by it?

In *Momentum*, Eric skillfully reveals the insights that are enabling him to be successful. Some of these insights will be new to you. Others are not new but are presented in a way that is fresh. This book has life coming from its pages. You will enjoy it and benefit from it.

Eric believes there is more for us to experience, but not just haphazardly. He believes more is possible for those who are willing to humble themselves and walk in what they did not produce but have been given, and ride the *Momentum* of their spiritual inheritance.

STEVE THOMPSON
Catalyst—NU World Ministries
Author of *You May All Prophesy*

This great book affirms what I believe to be true about the significance of godly inheritance and the importance to honor those who have gone before us to continue generational blessing. *Momentum* is instructive and inspiring for such a mandate. It ignites a desire to go beyond any previous generation. It is a commission to do something great with what we have been given while contributing our own unique gifts and abilities to continue the momentum that God started centuries ago. Eric and Bill Johnson's revelation on inheritance and the way they have lived it out will empower you to run with momentum generationally. I thoroughly recommend this book.

RUSSELL EVANS
Founder and Director of Planetshakers Ministries
and Planetshakers City Church

CONTENTS

Foreword. 17

Introduction 21

CHAPTER 1 Heir Force—*Bill Johnson*. 25

CHAPTER 2 All I Have Is Yours 43

CHAPTER 3 Possessing Your Inheritance. 57

CHAPTER 4 Access Through Honor—*Bill Johnson*. 67

CHAPTER 5 Forever and Ever. 77

CHAPTER 6 Inheriting the Supernatural—*Bill Johnson*. 97

CHAPTER 7 Grafted Into the Family 113

CHAPTER 8 Living in Extreme Security. 125

CHAPTER 9 Inheritance Promotes Us to Responsibility 137

CHAPTER 10 Developing Powerful People 151

CHAPTER 11 The End Game—*Bill Johnson*. 167

MOMENTUM
MOMENTUM
MOMENTUM
MOMENTUM
MOMENTUM

FOREWORD

The Father/Son paradigm is the centerpiece of God's Kingdom and God's whole plan for man on earth. This pivotal fact has been hidden from us in plain sight—in history by its absence and in the Bible by its presence. Of all the names Jesus could have called God, He called Him "Father," first when He was twelve years of age and then throughout His ministry. His essential identity was as the Son of God. God's essential identity was as Father. God's great declaration at the baptism of Jesus was, "This is My beloved Son, in whom I am well pleased!" How have we missed this strategic connection? The absence of it has brought a curse; the recovery of it will bring immediate and untold blessing.

Enter Bill and Eric Johnson, father and son, speaking of inheritance—the privileges and expressions of fatherhood and sonship. This is none other than the creative foundation of God's plan for the cosmos. God had in mind a family, and that family would be the model, the driving force of the Kingdom of the heavens, the culture of God.

I have been a "Bethel watcher" for more than a decade and have been privileged to visit Redding, California, in several capacities from a visiting speaker in the church, teacher in the School of Supernatural Ministry, to just "hanging out" around the campus, offices, healing rooms, and prayer ministry. This book is what I expected to be born of one of the most amazing and extended works of God in the entire world. There is an identifiable secret to what is being expressed at Bethel. If one is looking for something complex, the result is bound to be disappointment. The secret is contained in one word—*family*—and expressed in two words: *fathers* and *sons.* Bill and Eric recognize the centrality of inheritance and seek to give it face, hands, feet, and body as well as a voice. Echoes from Psalm 2 are being sounded across the whole, wide world: *"You are My Son; today I have become Your Father.... Pay homage to the Son"* (Ps. 2:7,12 Holman).

This book deals with what was prophesied in Malachi 4:5-6:

> *Look, I am going to send you Elijah the prophet before the great and awesome Day of the LORD comes. And he will turn the hearts of fathers to [their] children and the hearts of children to their fathers. Otherwise, I will come and strike the land with a curse* (Holman).

What is written in Malachi 4:5-6 is being fulfilled this very hour in places like Bethel Church in Redding, California, and in people like Bill and Eric Johnson. This is a frontline book on a frontline subject featuring a frontline father and son. It is happening across the world, and it's working! It's working because it's what God had in mind from the beginning. It was right then, and it is right now!

The idea of this book is right.

The content of this book is right.

The vast potential of this book is right!

All this because God was right from the beginning about family, and a proper climax to this whole, wonderful experience of time, space, light, and life is impossible without it.

Thank you, Bill and Eric, father and son, for sounding an early trumpet toward the great revival of the eternal paradigm featuring Father and Sons, Inc., God's Forever Family Business.

JACK TAYLOR, President
Dimensions Ministries
Melbourne, Florida

MOMENTUM
MOMENTUM
MOMENTUM
MOMENTUM
MOMENTUM

INTRODUCTION

*I must study politics and war that my sons may have
liberty to study mathematics and philosophy.*

—JOHN ADAMS

When I set out to write this book, it came from a desire to communicate to the Body of Christ an awareness of the privilege and responsibility of the Kingdom. I long to see a generation of people come to a fuller understanding of who God is and be drawn into His mysteries. One of the common issues I see is that we have allowed our own life experiences and circumstances to define who God is in a way that minimizes Him. As a result of this, we have created doctrines and theologies that keep the true Gospel hidden. So, in turn, Christians across the planet are not able to walk in the awareness of who God is and what He intends to do. This ultimately has created a misrepresentation of the Gospel.

One thing we do know is that Jesus fully and perfectly represented the Kingdom. He was so successful at accomplishing this not only because of the power and authority He had, but also because of His awareness and relationship with His Father. This perfect union made it possible for Him to fully and accurately represent the power of the Gospel. As He put it, "I only do what I see the Father doing" (see John 5:19). He was unashamed that He got His success from His Father. *Unashamed!*

It is my desire to help restore our understanding of *spiritual inheritance.* The challenge with mentioning the word *inheritance* rests with each reader's own understanding of inheritance. If someone doesn't think he has an inheritance, then the response will be, "It's not relevant to me." I often encounter Christians who truly believe that they have little or no inheritance and blessings coming from God, so they remove themselves from living as sons or daughters of the King. This book confronts that paradigm. It's also for those who know they have an inheritance and want to see it increase for the next generation.

The validity of inheritance, along with the momentum that it is capable of creating, is of extreme importance. The things that are taking place across the globe today and the speed at which the Kingdom is advancing are astounding. This momentum from inheritance is carrying us into unknown territory spiritually and physically, which is why we, the generation alive today, must make understanding inheritance a high priority. A generation yet unborn is depending on you and me to set the stage for them. But here's the deal: the stage can only be set for them if we embrace the stage that has been set for us.

Tapping into this momentum will alter the course of your life and the lives of those around you. It's impossible for it not to. History has shown us that only a few people have understood inheritance in its purest form, and since it's only a few, we have created a theology that what they experienced was a "sovereign" thing. The mystery of inheritance is being unraveled before our eyes as we realize all people have an inheritance. The sovereign plan was intended for all people—including you!

When I met with Don Milam from Destiny Image Publishing, we began to chat about this project, and a great idea came forth—for my dad to contribute to this book. He wrote four of the chapters (which are noted). It was very fitting not only because this topic of inheritance is strongly on both of our hearts, but also because inheritance is about generations. We thought it would be good to have both of our perspectives—father's and son's. It is such an honor to have my dad contribute to this book. Thanks, Dad!

Running with inheritance,
ERIC JOHNSON

CHAPTER 1

HEIR FORCE

BILL JOHNSON

While recently thumbing through an airline magazine, I saw a picture of a statue that caught my eye. It is of a muscular man with a hammer and chisel carving himself out of stone. It is a spectacular work by Colorado artist, Bobbie Carlyle, called the "Self-Made Man."

I love rags-to-riches stories. They are one of the positive attributes of a land with opportunities in which everyone has the chance to succeed. Such stories usually have a similar thread in that people, through discipline, determination, and hard work, accomplish things that no one in their families had accomplished before them. Whether economic, occupational, or based in sports, entertainment, or politics, the stories are inspiring.

"Self-made millionaire" is a common phrase used to describe a particular group of people who are greatly admired in our culture. They should be highly respected for their unusual accomplishment, assuming it was done with integrity. These kinds of people are usually more responsible with their resources because they know what it's like to have nothing. There's something to be said about the people who, having lived with little to nothing, learned how to appreciate much. Character is often forged in many hearts through this process. The children of Israel were trained in the wilderness through daily dependence on God for their provision. That prepared them for their inheritance of the Promised Land. God has similar lessons for us.

PRIVILEGED ABUSE

Inheritance has had much bad press because of a few who have abused the purpose of blessing. Modern history is filled with the stories of people inheriting millions of dollars and never having to work a day in their lives. Their pictures fill the tabloids as they pursue one pleasure after another. While there are certainly exceptions, the corruption that takes place in the hearts of many people with extraordinary privilege has become all too obvious. Many of society's saddest stories are of the privileged few who find little pleasure in what they already have. They often end up with broken homes or become drug addicts or drunks, and some even take their own lives. All of this comes to pass because of the failed pursuit of happiness. Society isn't so kind to those who have great privilege but ~~who~~ have not learned to steward their wealth responsibly with honor and dignity.

While most people would love a large financial inheritance, there exists in the subconscious mind a resistance to its purpose because of such abuses. And the Church has failed for centuries at receiving and utilizing the full inheritance promised to us through the Scriptures. Much like lottery winners, heirs to wealth often lose what they were given because they may have never been trained to manage the wealth they were to receive. Whenever the passion for pleasure is stronger than the passion for purpose and responsibility, there will always be a drain on resources, regardless of the size of the wealth or how it was obtained.

ENTITLEMENT, THE ENEMY OF BOTH RICH AND POOR

The safeguard for this journey is found in Jesus' instruction to be poor in spirit. Being poor in spirit is not being self-critical or condemning. It is the continual realization that every blessing in our lives is entirely because of God's grace. None of it is earned— even on our best days. It must also be noted that being poor in spirit is not being in spiritual poverty. Quite the opposite. It is the surest way to abundance in the things of the Spirit of God. In that frame of mind and heart, we know that every difficulty in life has a measure of God's grace available to bring about a victory. This posture, no matter how blessed we become, must be maintained throughout the growing process. To fail to do so is to choose where we stop in our growth. → consistent awareness the every good thing is from God's grace, not our works.

If either the rich or the poor are not poor in spirit, they become crippled with the spirit of entitlement. The poor feel the government owes them a life of success without needing to work for it, while the rich believe their wealth entitles them to special treatment by laws, courts, and government officials. The same trap is set for both groups who reject the invitation to become poor in spirit. They both taste of poverty in the worst possible way. That way of life destroys and wreaks havoc in the hearts of people who are positioned by God for greatness. Spiritual poverty is ensured when we reject the process to become poor in spirit. This must be understood, as spiritual inheritance affords us options that were never available previously.

Ms. Carlyle profoundly got her point across with her statue of the "Self-Made Man." Yet what this says of our culture is alarming. Whether this was her intention or not, I don't know. Regardless, it reveals how people think when there is little-to-no consciousness of God, our Creator.

A verse comes to mind that has a huge effect on my outlook on life: *"The horse is prepared for the day of battle, but victory belongs to the LORD"* (Prov. 21:31 NASB). One of the more dangerous parts of life is revealed in this statement. It is one thing to see the hand of God when something impossible happens before our eyes. It's quite another to see His hand when we've worked hard to bring something about through our own gifts, insights, and efforts. It is vital to give God the glory even when everyone around us thinks we earned it through our devotion and hard work.

"Self-made" people sometimes accomplish much in our eyes, but not in God's. We were designed to advance in every area of life through assistance and inheritance. In other words, it is impossible to reach the potential heights of personal development and in turn impact the world around us as self-made people. Some things are only possible through inheritance.

SELF-IMPOSED RESTRICTIONS

Wealth has a divine purpose that few can manage well. Correct management is a series of wise choices that come from a healthy heart. Proverbs is a gift from God for those who desire to live well by making such choices. The writer of Proverbs, by the Holy Spirit, gives a promise and a warning to the person of excellence:

> *Do you see a man skilled in his work? He will stand before kings; he will not stand before obscure men. When you sit down to dine with a ruler, consider carefully what is before you, and put a knife to your throat if you are a man of great appetite* (Proverbs 22:29; 23:1-2 NASB).

This passage speaks to the fact that people of excellence will influence kings. Those who will stand before kings also get a warning as to what tool the devil will use to end their place of influence with the mighty: they must recognize their own tendency to desire the material things, title, and position that they become exposed to in their new place of influence. The biblical answer seems rather harsh. But it gets the point across. We must "put a knife to our throats" if we are attracted to the things we don't have. This is what good management does. It has the wisdom to use self-imposed restrictions wherever and whenever needed. This is the ability to manage our internal world. And when we see that we have a tendency toward something that could destroy the place of influence, we use self-discipline to stay safe and effective.

Thoughts, attitudes, and desires reveal the heart's condition. Paying attention to these things is not to bring shame or condemnation. It is to bring wisdom so we know how to navigate through the various parts of life and handle them successfully. Managing our internal world really is the prerequisite for increased external blessing and influence.

CHOOSING CHARACTER

Wealth and favor, which is power, is in the purpose of God for His people. It's what is behind His system of promotion, honor, and reward. Yet, in history, few have lived well under its burden. Character is the only suitable container for such privilege. And only seasoned character will work when there is extreme privilege.

Obtaining such power in God's Kingdom is not through the means parroted by Wall Street and this world's system. It is not by striving for more. It is by serving, giving, denying self, surrender, and so forth. When John said to *"love not the world"* (1 John 2:15 KJV), he was specifically addressing our attachment and love for this world's system that works apart from divine influence. It actually undermines the purposes of His Kingdom.

Just as there were two trees in the Garden of Eden, there are two basic choices given to the wealthy: power for self exaltation, resulting in destruction; or power to contribute to the well-being of others and enable them to come into fulfillment, purpose, and destiny. To miss this is to "gain the whole world, but lose your own soul" (see Matt. 16:26). Yet the subject of this book is not actually money, nor is it even financial inheritance. It is entirely spiritual. But as Jesus taught powerful spiritual truths through money and nature, so we can learn much by examining natural parallels to the wonderful subject of spiritual inheritance. As I do this, please keep in mind that *neither financial lack nor abundance is an accurate measure of our spirituality.*

AMBITION—HOLY OR UNHOLY

There is a right way and a wrong way of pursuing promotion and increase. For example, God warned Israel about their desire for a king. They wanted to be like other nations, which should have given them a clue that their ambitions were foolish. Their pursuit of an unholy "promotion" gave rise to rulers over them who mirrored the same unholy values Israel had in wanting a king. Israel reaped what they sowed (see Gal. 6:7). Using the tools of the wrong kingdom always leads to bondage and imprisonment.

You can't use the ways of the world's system and expect to inherit the benefits of God's Kingdom. God warned Israel that earthly kings would use their power to build up their own kingdoms and increase their personal bank accounts at the people's expense. Yet we know that kings were a part of God's plan. He gave a promise to Jacob, saying, *"…and kings shall come forth from you"* (Gen. 35:11 NASB). God obviously intended His kings to rule according to the values of Heaven and not just utilize their position for personal gain. But kings had to be made, not merely elected or appointed.

When Israel cried out for a king, Saul was the best available and was duly appointed. But he had not gone through the refinement needed to make him the king God intended. His character couldn't properly contain the privilege given to him. David, on the other hand, had years of discipline to prepare him for the job. He correctly represented God's intention for the position, perhaps more than any other king. Jesus, God's only Son, will be called the Son of David throughout eternity. David had won this place of influence in God's heart.

THE "BLESS ME CLUB"

It may seem that discussions of ruling, power, and influence are strange subjects in a book about spiritual inheritance. But they shouldn't be. Inheritance is power. It has a purpose that must be captured to be a benefit. *We must be blessed to be a blessing.*

It was the Holy Spirit who inspired the following prayer:

> *God be gracious to us and bless us, and cause His face to shine upon us. That Your way may be known on the earth, Your salvation among all nations…God blesses us, that all the ends of the earth may fear Him* (Psalm 67:1-2,7 NASB).

The fear of seeking blessing has cost us dearly. It is no doubt a reaction to those who have abused blessing and privilege. The failure to passionately pursue the blessing of God is perhaps the most acceptable selfish trait in the Church. And tragically, such failure has been called humility. Yet being blessed is one of the greatest witnessing tools we have. According to Psalm 67, it causes the world to find out what God is like, leading to salvation. Remember the Scripture says that it is His kindness that leads to repentance (see Rom. 2:4). It's one thing to speak about the goodness of the Lord, but it's quite another to model it. Perhaps it is His goodness upon our lives that is to arrest the world and convict them of their misaligned lives. The misuse of blessing has brought embarrassment and shame to the Church. But proper use brings mass conversions, impacting the nations of the world (see Ps. 67:2,7).

RULING OR SERVING

By God's design, kings were to be the "apostles" of the Old Testament—the least of all, for the benefit of all. They were to use their favor and resources to help others come into their destiny.

Healthy citizens always become contributors to society, hope-givers to humanity, and ones who bring glory to God through their lives of purity and power. Such is the role of a righteous king: to help build and raise up healthy citizens. And such is the role of a believer with an inheritance.

All government has two basic purposes. The first is to provide safety to its citizens. The second is to create the opportunity for success and personal fulfillment in an atmosphere of safety. Kings, then, are to be a benefit to the people in these two areas before anything else is accomplished.

Herein lies an interesting picture given through the Bible's instruction on leadership and influence. Biblical government is to rule *over* people without controlling or abusing them. But biblical government also comes *under* people to serve and empower them to their places in life without becoming a doormat through disrespect. *Over and under.* Both have a biblical basis. This tension is relieved as we see that God's leaders *rule over* people for safety, but *come under* people to empower.

Empowerment is a primary gift given to those with unlimited resource and favor. We need to look no further than Jesus, the King of all kings, to find the example to follow. This King washed the feet of those He discipled. In training them to do what He did, He then sent them out to use their newfound authority and power in serving others. Power and authority—two tools used to serve others, not to build personal kingdoms.

Jesus became the extreme example of this way of life. He was the first to model what He taught His disciples: "...to whom much is given, from him much will be required..." (see Luke 12:48). This was a charge given to those of special privilege. But many have become absorbed in the pursuit of pleasure through wealth, even though the richest man to ever live warned against it, saying,

"He who loves pleasure will become a poor man..." (Prov. 21:17 NASB). The pursuit of building personal empires is the surest way to break the cycle of blessing and to damage or weaken our legacy.

Inheritance is power. And this power must be directed toward Kingdom purposes through Kingdom attitudes and mindsets. A biblical inheritance positions us to have great impact on the nations of the world.

WHAT IS OUR INHERITANCE?

The concept of spiritual inheritance is not one that I think we have had great understanding of. Perhaps the misuse of inherited financial wealth by the privileged few has contributed to this form of resistance. And then again, it could be that we have just been ignorant of what God made available. Regardless, the Church has been reticent to embrace our responsibility to manage such spiritual wealth well. Yet God has given us everything necessary for us to accomplish our assignment to disciple the nations of the world. Lack is never on His end of the equation.

Rather than draw conclusions based on our various cultures, or even our own experience or the lack thereof, let's look to the instruction given to us by God:

> *The secret things belong to the LORD our God, but the things revealed belong to us and to our sons forever, that we may observe all the words of this law* (Deuteronomy 29:29 NASB).

There are two parts to this verse that are important for us to consider: the value of mystery, and the value of revelation. Both are essential realities in the Christian life. *Mystery* represents things withheld from us by God. *Revelation* represents what God has given to us to be stewarded as a treasure. The latter is to be *passed on* as a permanent possession to our descendants, forever! This stunning statement carries a "snowball" effect in that its potential gets bigger and bigger throughout time. Because of that, it is truer today than in any previous day.

WONDERFUL MYSTERY!

Mystery is a beautiful subject for many reasons. But as it is not the primary focus of this study, I'll address it rather briefly. There are two parts to mystery that are important for us. First, we need to have areas in our lives that we have no understanding of so we can learn to trust God. If I understand everything about my Christian life, I have an inferior Christian life. What I don't understand is often as important as what I do. That becomes the grounds for the relationship of trust. Christianity is called "the Faith." As such, it must contain mystery.

Second, and this must be held in tension with the first, God has chosen to give us the realm of mystery as a gift. This basically means we have access to hidden things. Hunger and development of character are two essential elements to this process of searching out mysteries. Hunger is the driving force that enables us to take possession of what God has promised. And character provides the "container" to place the blessing in. The bottom line is that mystery is completely managed by God. It is not ours to demand or control. Yet our influence in the matter through dependence and hunger is seen in His delight to give us more than we could ever ask for.

"Jesus answered them, 'To you it has been granted to know the mysteries of the kingdom of heaven...'" (Matt. 13:11 NASB). He invites us into the pursuit of the hidden things. For He does not hide things *from* us as much as He hides things *for* us. Even the hidden things belong to us before they are revealed. It's important to remember that we will always be learning and expanding in wisdom throughout eternity, which means mystery will always exist. Having said that, today's mystery is tomorrow's revelation. Such is the pleasure of serving a God who is always good, but can never be fully comprehended.

PERSONAL REVELATION

Look at the phrase *things revealed* in Deuteronomy 29:29. Every generation has received a measure of revelation from God. Revelation is to lead to encounter. When it doesn't, we become bigger in our heads than we are in our hearts. God is to be experienced. Someone that significant is not to be known only through concept and principle.

Consider what this verse implies: Everything ever given to human beings by God, no matter how long ago or for what purpose, was to be passed on as an inheritance to their descendants. Practically speaking, what was given to Moses in his God encounters on the mountain was supposed to be passed on as an inheritance to his people forever. His personal experience opened the door for a nation's corporate experience.

King David was chief among worshipers. His insights and experiences in the glory were to become the standard by which a people learned to encounter God. The beauty of David's worship expression and how he navigated himself in the glory were supposed to be made available to all who followed.

Elijah is aptly called the prophet of power. His exploits against the enemies of Israel were legendary. Thus, his anointing became the prototype of John the Baptist, who prepared the way for Jesus Himself. Elijah's faith in God's power, his insights into the lifestyle of risk, and his abandonment to God's purposes were all to become standards by which the people of God lived ever since Elijah's death.

The list of those who made their mark with God is nearly endless. And each of them obtained something that was supposed to be inherited by the following generation and then built upon, reaching new heights in humankind's journey with God. It is tragic when each generation has to reinvent the wheel, so to speak, and discover for themselves something they could have received through an impartation through inheritance. The time spent in rediscovery could have been spent building upon what the previous generation left to inherit.

All of the heroes of both Scripture and history had something from God that was supposed to be passed on to their descendants. It says, *"...The things revealed belong to us **and to our sons forever...**"* (Deut. 29:29 NASB). And while we live under a measure of benefit from their experience, we still have not maintained many of these realms as an inheritance. Most of what we have is the memory or memorial of a previous accomplishment, not a sustained breakthrough with increase.

Consider at this point what it would look like to have an extremely wealthy businessman and woman raise their children with purpose, not to only inherit their wealth, but actually to be able to manage the money, business, and family vision with increase in mind. Money can be measured and is, therefore, a good tool to illustrate this principle. Wealthy parents know what they own and what they have to leave to their heirs.

We must learn how to live with a consciousness of personal breakthrough—what we "own" that can be passed on freely to those we impact with our lives. These wealthy parents are also painfully aware of what it takes to manage wealth. They live with intention because they live with conviction through knowledge gained by experience. The scars of sacrifice, discipline, and failure serve to remind them of the cost they paid for such increase.

The believer has all that and more. For this reason we must live aware of the fact that what God has done for us and through us was *all* by grace. In maintaining that heart attitude, we possess the conviction that these things are to be passed on to others. This is the "poor in spirit" mandate given to us by Jesus. It is an essential attitude in the lives of those receiving inheritance.

As it was with David, who set one of the ultimate "high water marks" for humanity, so it is for today's believer. David killed the lion and the bear when no one was watching. It qualified him to beat Goliath when two nations were watching. Our private victories are to become public blessings. Such is the process of building an inheritance.

The implication is that inheritance is to be passed on from one generation to another. Everything that humanity has ever learned from God was given by revelation and encounter. That very thing was never taken back into the heavenly realm by God, but was left here to be inherited by the following generation.

ATTRACT TO EQUIP

In every generation, men and women of God rise to the top because of the gifting and the favor on their lives. Many of them attract crowds wherever they go. They use their gift to inspire the Church through their gift and often bring multitudes to Christ. But when their gift is used only to inspire instead of equip and release, people admire the gift, but are never able to emulate anything similar to this one they admire.

It's not that we as leaders are to create clones of our personalities and gifts. It's just that gifts from God are to be released for the whole Body to benefit from. What once caused a person to stand out as an unusually gifted person should become the new standard for the Body of Christ through the process of equipping the saints. This is spiritual inheritance made practical. It happens *directly* through training, discipleship, and impartation, and *indirectly* through honor, respect, study, and prayer.

That is what Moses meant when he said, *"...Would that all the LORD's people were prophets, that the LORD would put His Spirit upon them!"* (Num. 11:29 NASB). Joshua was jealous for Moses because others were doing what only Moses was known to do. Moses correctly adjusted Joshua's thinking. In doing so, he prophesied of a future day when the Spirit would be released upon all God's people, creating a new standard for what could be accomplished by the average believer. This means that the extraordinary anointing upon one would become the possession and experience of all. This has incomprehensible possibilities.

I personally get nauseated over those who claim to have the mantle of Smith Wigglesworth or any other hero of the faith. First of all, if it were true, let someone else say it. It should never be our claim to make. Second, the goal is not for us to be identified by the nature of another person's gift. It is to draw and build upon previous breakthroughs so that we can step into the full purpose of God for us and for our generation. God doesn't want or need another Wigglesworth, as great as he was. He wants you and me, as we are, surrendered to His purposes, utilizing the breakthroughs of the generations that have gone before us to accomplish something new.

What He has planned for us is much bigger than we think—and impossible to achieve through determination alone. In fact, it will take the sanctified efforts of multiple generations to accomplish our God-given assignment. It's even bigger than the need for unity among the generations that are privileged to be alive at the same time. It will take a rediscovery of the concept of *spiritual inheritance* through the unity of generations past and present. This is done only through true unity of the Spirit, for He alone knows the intended heartbeat of each generation.

THE ULTIMATE EARTHLY INHERITANCE

There were kings who followed after David who received special treatment from God simply because they were his descendants. David had obtained such a place of victory and favor before God that it became a corporate blessing, both to those under his rule and those in the generations to follow. Tragically, most of the succeeding kings didn't value the inheritance they received and got caught up in the power and privilege of their position.

An inheritance gives people an advantage, if they will use it correctly. But it will cost them dearly if they don't. These descendants of David started life with position and great favor with God. Favor with God is the greatest inheritance, apart from the actual presence of God. It is money in the bank in the Kingdom economy. But as it is in the natural, so it is in the spiritual. Having money in the bank doesn't mean I will use it correctly. And many have suffered shipwreck due to mismanagement of spiritual inheritance.

Preachers' kids are notorious for sinful and rebellious behavior. Is it possible that they are a primary target for the powers of darkness because of the favor they carry and their position to be in line for an inheritance to build upon? Their access to spiritual inheritance is a great threat to the dark realm. And so, like the privileged few who inherit millions and live without restraint, this special breed of people gets sidetracked from their purpose.

Sometimes they miss their call because of a double standard that is lived in the preacher's home. It ends up undermining the destiny of the children. If they see one message preached from the pulpit and quite another lived at home, they use the discrepancy as the justification to abandon the life of faith preached by the parents. And then again, it is sometimes caused by church members who play right into the devil's hands through their criticisms and unsanctified requirements placed on the children of men and women of God. The stories of such failures are, regretfully, many.

Thankfully, the stories of success are on the increase as the awareness of the principle of inheritance is growing. Religion is form without power. It is cruel and boring and has taken the lives of many young people who had great potential in God. Inheritance reveals purpose. We are blessed to live at a time when the tide is turning and more and more people are learning how to capitalize on their place in life. And more and more *descendants of the mighty* are in fact rising to their potential.

CHAPTER 2

ALL I HAVE IS YOURS

We are not allowed to apologize for something that has been given to us for free.

—Pastor Judah Smith

ALL I HAVE IS YOURS

It was a normal hot day in the field. The familiar smell of sweat and dust filled the air as the hustling and bustling noises of a growing city echoed over the horizon. The temperature was still climbing as the sun was beginning to peak in the pale blue sky. With a hoe in hand and bag of seeds on the hip, his goal today was to finish seeding this small corner of the field.

Another sound began to fill the air. It was a different sound; however, it was recognizable. The man stood up straight and leaned on his hoe and pointed his ears in the direction of the sound. As he listened, it reminded him of his dad's guitar, and those drums... they were his that he had received many years ago. Drawing closer to the music, he dropped the hoe, and, curious as to why music was coming from his father's villa, broke into a light jog, eager to find out what all the celebration was about.

As he approached the courtyard, he noticed the dirt and sweaty smell was now replaced with a smell of freshly cooked meat along with some freshly cut vegetables from their community garden. The man was trying to figure out if he had forgotten somebody's birthday, anniversary, or wedding. He went through the list in his head and realized he hadn't forgotten any important dates. Now his curiosity was turning into confusion as he scanned the courtyard. He quickly identified some family members and the little children chasing or being chased by each other.

On the backside of the courtyard was a large table that was only used for special occasions. As he looked at the faces that sat at this table, his attention was instantly drawn to the one sitting at the head of the table. His confusion turned into anger. *How could this be?* He then looked around to find his father. His father was now just walking out of the villa with his best robe and brand-new pair of sandals and a small box. What happened next was absolutely shocking.

You see, the young man sitting at the head of the table was his younger brother. Two full moons ago in this very courtyard, a major argument had taken place near the fountain. Words were said that are too embarrassing and cruel to repeat. This younger brother did the unthinkable and told his father, "I wish you were dead so I could have my inheritance." It was a very sad night for this family. The father, in his pain, decided to give his youngest son his inheritance. After the big argument, the younger brother left and headed north, and for the last two months, he had spent his entire inheritance on anything that fulfilled the lust of his flesh.

As the father approached the head of the table, he asked his youngest son to please stand. As he stood, the father took his best robe and placed it on his back. Then he knelt down and grabbed each foot and put on the new sandals that he had purchased the day after the big argument two moons ago. Then he stood back up and opened the small wooden box that was on the table. The father pulled out a ring. This wasn't any normal ring; it was the *family* ring. He grabbed his son's right hand and placed the ring on his finger. In sheer excitement the father exclaimed, "My son is home." A great cheer went out that could be heard for miles around.

The man from the field was now beet red in the face; his fist clenched as if he were ready for a fight. He couldn't hold back anymore and started yelling, "Father, I have spent my entire life working for you, and you have never done anything like this for me!"

Now the party went completely silent, and all eyes were fixed on the man and the father. All you could hear was the angry man's heavy breathing and the soft sound of water from the fountain. The father looked at the man and said, "Son, your younger brother was lost, but he is now found."

Then the man replied firmly, "But Dad, he ridiculed and embarrassed you and our family. I have never embarrassed you, and now you throw a big party for him."

What the father said next revealed something that the man had never realized in his entire life: "Son, you are always with me, and I am always with you. All that I have is yours."

The man took off running into the night, and now he was more confused than ever. As he ran, he replayed what had just happened over and over in his head. All these memories of childhood came flooding into his mind. He simply became overwhelmed by the confusing nature of what had just happened. He ran for a while until the sound of his footsteps was all he could hear. Now he found himself slumping over a large boulder, gasping for air and searching for answers.

All he could hear was what his father said before he ran into the night: "All that I have is yours." For the first time in his life he realized he didn't know what it meant to walk in his inheritance. Right then he made a decision to spend the rest of his life learning what that means.

THE FAMILY BUSINESS

Something that we fully grasp can be the very thing that creates a momentum that will touch a generation that we will never see. It's paramount that we seek to understand and take hold of our inheritance. History is not just meant to be celebrated; it is meant to be the floor we stand on. Let us be a generation that accomplishes what is unprecedented.

In our modern culture, individualism is a value system embraced by many. An individualistic mindset, in more ways than we think, can lead people to reject something that was already there—*inheritance*. Individualism outside of a family and community can become very divisive and damaging.

Let's take, for example, a family business. The father and mother have given their lives to building it, and it has become successful over time. Since this business is successful, they have had to hire employees as the business expands, and one of the hires is their daughter. As she begins to settle into her new job, there is a good chance she will get the feeling from other employees that she only has a job because her dad and mom own the place. What she does at this point is really important. Her reaction will show the state of her identity.

If she allows this pressure from the other employees to get the best of her, she will begin to "perform" and "prove" to others that she deserves this job. Let's first take a look at the pressure to perform. This is what it would look like. She would probably show up to work early and even work longer and harder than her co-workers, all for the purpose of showing that she is serious about her job. If she did something successful in relation to her job, she would make sure that her co-workers knew about it. This would all be done to show them that she deserves this job based on her performance.

Let's say that she doesn't want to perform, but instead wants to prove to everybody that she is fully capable of doing it by herself and doesn't need her parents' help. What she will probably do is move across town and start a business of her own. When this business becomes successful over time and has grown into a bona fide business that is contributing economically to that city, she will have proven to everybody that she is fully capable of doing it on her own. So, instead of stepping into the momentum her parents created for her, she has decided to do it on her own and start from square one.

A huge part of our modern culture pushes us to generate new ideas and to work hard and stake our place in the world by our own merit. If what drives us to neglect an inheritance and start something on our own comes out of this desire to perform or prove, then it is a mistake to start something new for that purpose. We would be geniuses to learn how to push through the urge to perform or prove and to move into a place of building on what's been given to us.

Now please understand, there is nothing wrong with working harder or starting something new. The real question isn't what we do. It's why we're doing what we're doing. Too many times we have made decisions that are based out of a poverty mindset, which causes us to perform or prove our way into a place of influence when all the while we are being given access through inheritance and heritage. If accessed correctly, inheritance will allow us to accomplish more than we could ever dream of doing on our own.

It's important to look at what a poverty mindset is. *Merriam-Webster* gives this definition of the word *poverty:*

> 1: *a:* the state of one who lacks a usual or socially ac-ceptable amount of money or material possessions *b:* re-nunciation as a member of a religious order of the right as an individual to own property 2: scarcity, dearth 3 *a:* debility due to malnutrition *b:* lack of fertility[1]

When we have a poverty mindset, we live in an awareness of what's lacking. For example, pride is what drives the poverty mindset. A poverty mindset creates a powerful illusion that everything is about us. Awareness of the state of lack in our lives tends to cause us to become self-centered and believe we are help-less victims. When we live in this lie, we put the responsibility of our lives on someone else or God and never fully take ownership of ourselves.

Common statements from the poverty mindset sound like this: "It's not my fault." "Why doesn't someone do this for me?" This begins to create an environment of thoughts and ideas that cause people never to fully take responsibility for what's been given to them. If we can't take ownership for our own lives, it's nearly impossible to know what to do with something that has been given to us for free. It is extremely important to confront any type of poverty mindset that is operating in our lives.

Let's go back to our illustration of the family-owned business. Now if the daughter decides not to perform or prove herself in this position and moves into embracing her inheritance, something historical is about to take place. She will now experience a momentum that is dreamed about. Instead of a plot of dirt to build on, she will have a solid foundation waiting for her.

As a generation of people begins to recognize the inheritance they have, they will begin to rise, and in that rising, their level of interaction with the generation that gave them the inheritance will increase. This is what we call transition. While this transition is taking place, an incredible opportunity is at hand. How they navigate this transition will reveal what their true identity is. If their identity is healthy, they will prosper and augment the inheritance they have received. However, if their identity is on crutches, they will perform or demote themselves and actually sabotage their inheritance. Interestingly, many times people do this without even knowing what they are doing. They tend to do it in the name of humility.

It's really important for us to understand that inheritance is never about what we have done. It's all about who we are. We are not responsible for the fact that we got an inheritance. As soon as we can move away from the reasons we received an inheritance and start focusing on what we are going to do about what we've been given, some amazing things will take place.

We are not responsible for what we've been given as much as we are responsible for what we do with what we've been given. As Pastor Judah Smith has said, "We are not allowed to apologize for something that has been given to us for free."[2]

This pressure that the daughter faced is similar to what we face from day to day. If we make decisions that are performance-based, they can dramatically interfere with something that God set into motion from the beginning of humankind: our ability to build upon not just what we have worked so hard for, but what has been given to us for free.

I am often reminded of something that is a huge part of the reason I am who I am today. It has been a foundation for my family and me to stand on and has created opportunities that continue to amaze us. At the same time, it is very humbling. This thing is called *heritage*. My children are seventh-generation Christians on my dad's side of the family and fifth-generation on my mom's side of the family.

Something that has always fascinated me is how families with a rich heritage function. When people have a heritage, which creates a momentum that flows from one generation to the next, a dynamic takes place that is often missed by the naked eye. At some point, the younger generation begins to get involved in what the older generation has established. It occurs when the new generation recognizes the inheritance they are stepping into. When this is navigated correctly, it can increase the momentum that flows from the heritage. If it's not, then ultimately they lose what was meant for them.

There are several levels of our relationship with God. Often we find in the Bible statements that we are called "servants" of God (see Rom. 6:22). In the Old Testament, Moses was called a friend of God (see Exod. 33:11). This has become a personal desire of mine—that I wouldn't just be a servant of God, but would also be known as a friend of God.

There is quite a difference between being a servant and being a friend. Servants are more concerned about doing what they're supposed to do, and friends are more concerned about what they've been given and how to run with it. It seems that most believers are stuck in the servant mode. They have been given the green light to become a friend, yet they prefer to stay a servant. In Scripture, the nation of Israel had been given a chance to experience the glory of God on the mountain, but instead remained in the valley and sent Moses up (see Exod. 20:18-20). This is a great example of not taking advantage of what they had access to—a genuine relationship with God.

There is absolutely nothing wrong with being a servant as the Bible is very clear on the importance of being a servant and always serving. Jesus demonstrated that so well. In order to be a great friend, you have to learn to be a great servant.

You have many types of relationships: acquaintances, mutual friends, relatives, close friends, and so forth. You interact with your close friends completely differently than you would with a friend. That's because you are aware of the access you have to each other, so you can trust that level of connection to begin to be involved in each other's lives. When believers become aware of what they have access to through friendship with God, watch out! Something beautiful is taking place.

A CULTURE OF INHERITANCE

One of the things that we need to do to allow inheritance to flow from generation to generation is to create a culture where inheritances are legal and welcomed. A core part of a culture of inheritance lies in our ability to be able to celebrate someone else's greatness, anointing, and victories. As we cultivate this in our everyday lives as individuals and communities, we will experience a new level of momentum and flow from Heaven that is unprecedented.

It is common and very easy for us to celebrate and encourage people who work really hard and receive the fruits of their labor. If a farmer goes out into the field, plants seeds, and waters and watches over those seeds every day, eventually those seeds will turn into plants. Nobody would tell that farmer that he didn't deserve it. We would all say to that farmer, "Good job. You deserve it because you planted and watered those seeds, and that gives you the right to the fruit that comes of it." This is expected and normal when someone works hard—and gives them the right to access the fruits of their labor. Throughout the Book of Proverbs, it is clear that people should not be lazy, but should work hard and enjoy the fruits of their labor. This is a very important principle in Scripture and in life:

> *I went past the field of the sluggard, past the vineyard of someone who lacks judgment; thorns had come up everywhere, the ground was covered with weeds, and the stone wall was in ruins. I applied my heart to what I observed and learned a lesson from what I saw: a little sleep, a little slumber, a little folding of the hands to rest—and poverty will come on you like a bandit and scarcity like an armed man* (Proverbs 24:30-34 NIV).

One of the unique things about a true culture of inheritance is that jealousy and envy do not fuel that environment. I can go into any environment, and as I interact with the people in that environment, it doesn't take long for me to see what is fueling that environment: celebration, or jealousy and envy. Something that is rare to find is a culture or environment that celebrates and encourages when someone receives something that they didn't work for—an inheritance. In other words, it isn't the fruit of their own labor, but of someone else's labor. A typical reaction is, "What did they do to deserve that?" or "I have worked hard for what they got for free!" If we are going to establish a culture where inheritance and momentum are encouraged, then we need to stop asking the question why and start stewarding what we have in front of us.

When we are driven by performance, we will most likely have a challenge celebrating someone else's inheritance. We have created a lifestyle that is perpetuated by the level of performance we put out. So when we see other people get something they did nothing for, it violates our core value of performance. This causes some to perform more; for others, it may be the very thing that has stunted their spiritual growth.

The spirit that rejected Jesus at Nazareth is the same spirit that is unable to celebrate someone else (see Matt. 13:53-58). The people of Nazareth were familiar with Jesus. When we are familiar with people, we tend to no longer celebrate what we see in them. Often familiarity will breed doubt and jealousy. In this particular situation, Jesus was only able to do a few miracles. That's quite amazing—a city unknowingly determined the level of the supernatural by their inability to celebrate Jesus.

An incredible thing takes place when we embrace the opportunity to celebrate someone else's inheritance or momentum. Our hearts become shaped in a way that echoes the very heart of God. A culture where this is embraced will usher in momentum and create an atmosphere in which people, relationships, and ideas can thrive.

The Church has yet to be known purely as a place where we administer and celebrate life. For where there is death, the Church can bring life: Dysfunctional marriages can be restored to healthy marriages; disease-stricken bodies can be made completely whole and healthy; strife can be replaced with peace; and anger can be uprooted by joy. This is what it means to administer and celebrate life. That day approaches more quickly than ever, and we will be known as a place where we celebrate life and administer it to the world. I dream of a day when all over the world we hear more about people living life to its fullest and experiencing the beauty of God in everything they do.

When we become aware of someone else's greatness, anointing, and victories, it also exposes the attitudes of our hearts. Oh, what a beautiful thing! I can't help but think of the words, "create in me a clean heart," and the opportunities we will get when we pray that prayer. Our expectation for a clean heart is that we assume God will instantly make it clean. In my experience, it's a process of opportunities. In these opportune moments, we can make adjustments in our attitudes that calibrate our hearts to become and remain pure and clean.

It is important that we are diligent in creating a culture and environment where this concept of inheritance is legal and healthy—not just in theory, but also in practice. The key is to understand that each one of us has an inheritance, to make sure that our identity is intact, and to be more concerned with what God thinks and says than what people think and say.

When we base our level of worth on what people say, we will experience erratic, unstable lives. We have positioned ourselves to ebb and flow with the value that people have put on us. The moment we begin to let the value that God has put on us be our reference point, a shift takes place: Circumstances then cannot shape us; rather, we shape circumstances.

Our identity is to not be tied into what we do or to our surroundings; it is to be tied solely to the Creator. It is from the Creator that true identity comes. God not only created the universe, He gave everything an identity from which it is to operate. Apart from this identity, we will fall short of the fullness that He intended.

When we're operating from our true identity, we will find that pressure no longer controls what we do. This is why we can look at certain people around us and notice that they cannot be knocked off their horse. They remain the same regardless of the circumstances. This is very evident in the life of Jesus; He demonstrates so well what is possible for every believer. What a powerful place from which to live!

ENDNOTES

1. *Merriam-Webster's Collegiate Dictionary*, 11th ed., s.v. "poverty."

2. Judah Smith, quotation from an email to Eric Johnson on December 14, 2010.

CHAPTER 3

POSSESSING YOUR INHERITANCE

A few years ago, while flying to Alaska to do a conference, I was caught up in a conversation with the Lord. I had been pondering why kingdoms or empires fall. Why do we look into history and see a king build up his empire and then see it fall when the next generation takes over? Why do we see revival explode in one generation and then die in the next? As I was dwelling on these questions, I was led to read Numbers 13-14.

Israel had just left Egypt and now crossed the desert to their Land of Promise. In this moment in history, we can look at a nation that was in a huge season of change. They were on a journey that God set up to enable them to possess their inheritance. We can extract some keys from their story to help us navigate our current and coming transition in the years to come. We read in Numbers 13:1-3,

And the LORD spoke to Moses, saying, "Send men to spy out the land of Canaan, which I am giving to the

children of Israel; from each tribe of their fathers you shall send a man, every one a leader among them." So Moses sent them from the Wilderness of Paran according to the command of the LORD, all of them men who were heads of the children of Israel (Numbers 13:1-3).

Moses sends the spies into the Promised Land with some instructions. They were to come back and tell Moses and the nation of Israel what they had seen with their eyes and to bring back fruit from the land. This is very strategic in that it was to create an opportunity for the hearts of the nation to be revealed. As the spies return to camp, they begin to report what they have seen and show the fruit they found on the other side of the river.

The report they brought back of what they saw was that the land was already occupied and that there were giants there, too. Along with that report, they brought back different types of fruit and said the land was flowing with milk and honey. These two reports provoked an incredible tension in the hearts of Israel. Here they have a promise that the land is theirs, but at the same time it requires something they weren't expecting. It was an opportunity for them to position themselves to take possession of the land. But it was this price that they weren't able to pay.

A FRUIT-DRIVEN LIFE

What is fruit? According to *Merriam-Webster*, it is "a succulent plant part"; it also means "the effect or consequence of an action or operation."[1] In the natural sense, when we eat apples, we are eating what an apple tree worked to produce. In the spiritual sense, when we contend and steward what we are given, we will experience in those areas breakthrough, which is also called fruit. What is a report? It is an account of the facts and the things that we see and hear. For the sake of context, I am going to call it *reality*.

What I have found in my own life is that often in life we will receive a reality report and fruit at the same time. For example, for a number of years now at Bethel Church, we have been experiencing tremendous breakthrough in many areas of sickness, disease, and ailments. One area that we have intentionally targeted is cancer. We absolutely hate cancer with a passion.

Early on in this pursuit of declaring our city a "cancer-free zone," we did not see as much breakthrough as we do now. In this journey as a community of believers, there have been some great losses along the way, as well as great successes. A decision was made a long time ago that we would always keep our eyes on the fruit and not let the reality of cancer determine what we do. In other words, we have kept our eyes on what God was doing and not gotten distracted by what was not happening.

So instead of letting the reality of the strength of cancer in our world determine what we do, instead of looking at the fact that there "are giants in the land," we have chosen to look at the fruit because the fruit is an invitation to own the land it came from. At the same time when we lost battles to cancer, we were also seeing people healed of cancer. It was in this tension that we refused to equally value the report and the fruit.

With fruit comes responsibility. Any time we have equal affection for the fruit and the report, we create options. When we make options, we become divided. Many times we don't realize the effect this simple decision has in our daily lives. This type of decision has caused us to cope with the problem rather than taking a stance that is directly aimed at defeating the problem. We can see from experience that when we cope with something long enough, it begins to become our identity, and our ambition to defeat it becomes less. We then forget the problem is even there. Immunity sets in; it becomes normal, and we become accustomed to it.

This is where we fall into the trap. Rarely does this happen overnight. It usually takes place over time. This is important because, once we have been given fruit, we then need to move into a place of responsibility in stewarding it. There has to be an adjustment of attitude and affection from that day forward. We often wonder why God can't just give us everything we need without us needing to fight for anything. When we have to pay a price for something, it will then be of incredible value to us, and then we not only have the ability to pick the fruit any time we want, we also have the authority to administer it.

God's intention when He shows us the fruit is to lure us into a Kingdom reality where we can pick this fruit any time we want. When the nation of Israel saw the fruit, they had an opportunity to believe that God wanted them to live in the land it came from so they could have it any time they wanted. We can always tell if we own the Promised Land when we can pick the fruit any time we want. Instead, the Israelites decided to be distracted by the bad report.

I personally know a few individuals who own *promised land* in a spiritual sense. Some own the "financial" land and seem to always do well, and whatever they get involved with does really well financially. Because of this principle, they have allowed the fruit of that land to lead them to a place of owning it. For others, it's authority over diseases; their success rate for certain diseases and illnesses is very high. For the same reason, they have allowed the fruit to lead them to a place of authority over these diseases and sicknesses.

For most of them, it didn't come to them in a moment where all of a sudden they had all this authority over something. For many it started with a small breakthrough, or maybe they heard a testimony of breakthrough. The fruit could be as small as a grape, or it could be as big as a watermelon. No matter what size it is, it's still fruit. Often we have certain expectations of breakthrough, and when we don't see it happen to the level that we expected, we tend to overlook something that really is the key for greater breakthrough. So we must learn to recognize fruit no matter how big or small.

How do we begin to create a lifestyle that is fruit-driven and not reality-driven? First, we must develop an appetite for fruit. When we create an appetite for fruit, a hunger is created in us for that very thing. We begin to aim our affection, actions, and attention to attaining more fruit. Such a hunger is birthed in us that we're not satisfied that someone else is enjoying the fruit and we're not. We begin to make decisions and live lives that are in a constant pursuit of seeing that the Kingdom of Heaven is invading earth.

Our core value needs to be that God intended us to enjoy the fruit all the time. Psalm 68:19 states that He *"daily loads us with benefits."* God's desire is that we eat all the time. The Church has a tendency to believe that the fruit is for us to enjoy for a single moment; we don't realize it is bait that is meant to lure us to the source.

Let's start by recognizing the different times when we have had fruit show up in our lives and make the decision that we're after the land that it came from, while not allowing the bad report or the giants to deter us from the course. Let's give God permission to set us on a journey through the land of giants so we can own the real estate all those fruit trees are sitting on.

For Israel, the report was bigger in their eyes than the grapes that were brought back. They didn't realize that they had overlooked the fruit. Why did they overlook the fruit? Their expectation of the Promised Land was that they were just going to walk into the land to occupy it. A lot of times we get discouraged because our own expectation of how things should happen doesn't materialize, so we slow down or completely stop in the direction we are going. Little did the Israelites realize that they were required to win some victories to be able to occupy the land.

SHHHHHH! BE QUIET

As we read in Numbers 13:30, *"Then Caleb quieted the people before Moses, and said, 'Let us go up at once and take possession, for we are well able to overcome it.'"*

Here we see a pivotal moment taking place. We know the 12 spies had just finished their presentation to the people, and as a nation they chose to allow the bad report to dictate their next step. You can imagine the frustration and panic that began to spread throughout the camp. The realization set in that this Promised Land was going to require something of them—something they were not ready to do: face the giants! At this moment Caleb does something profound; he quiets the people and reminds them of the promise God gave them.

John Maxwell says, "A positional leader speaks first where real leaders speak later."[2] There is a lot of truth in this. You will find this trait in any good leader. It is this ability to know when to be silent and what to say when it's time to talk. Good leaders are very careful about what comes out of their mouths, and when it's the right moment, they know when to speak up. *"Death and life are in the power of the tongue, and those who love it will eat its fruit"* (Prov. 18:21).

The word *power* in Hebrew is *yad,* which means an extension or hand. It refers to a person's hand and the fact that we can arrange the world we live in. The idea is that with our tongues we have the ability and power to create the world that we live in. Essentially, what we speak forth will determine the quality of life we will experience. Many of us are unaware that the life we live now is the direct result of what we have said, yet we are surprised by it. Just because we *can* say it doesn't mean we *should.*

Ultimately, we create the atmosphere that we dwell in. What Caleb did was refuse to let panic and frustration create the atmosphere he was going to live in. He purposefully reminded the people that God had promised them this land and that His intention was for them to enter into that land.

We must ask ourselves this question: "What do I say when the pressure is on?" It is important to watch what we say when the pressure builds and we feel like we can't take it anymore. If we need help knowing what comes out of our mouths, we can ask a few people who know us best and find out from them. Ask them, "Do the attitudes of my heart and the words of my mouth bring life, or do they bring anxiety and stress?" Also, we should ask someone who is a new friend the same question. This will give us a decent snapshot on how the people around us see us.

This is a big deal because there are really bad days that come our way. In those moments, what we say reveals what's inside. If we can learn this art of being quiet and more careful with our words, we are ready to take on the giants. Learning to be quiet doesn't mean we become ignorant of the giants; it just means that we are not going to allow the pressure of the situation to cause us to create an atmosphere that is no fun to live in.

It is important to note that 40 years later in the Book of Joshua, when they are walking around Jericho just as God commanded, they also did something else that God didn't tell them to do and that was to "be quiet" and not to say a word while they walked around the city. The last time they opened their mouths, they had to go back to the wilderness for 40 years. They were making sure that wasn't going to happen again.

HINGING ON A PROMISE

Once Caleb quiets the people, he then begins to draw their attention to the most important thing in that moment—the *promise* the Lord had given them.

> *But Joshua the son of Nun and Caleb the son of Jephunneh, who were among those who had spied out the land, tore their clothes; and they spoke to all the congregation of the children of Israel, saying:* **"The land we passed through to spy out is an exceedingly good land. If the LORD delights in us, then He will bring us into this land and give it to us, 'a land which flows with milk and honey.'** *Only do not rebel against the LORD, nor fear the people of the land,* **for they are our bread;** *their protection has departed from them, and the LORD is with us. Do not fear them"* (Numbers 14:6-9).

This promise was meant to help them conquer the land. Imagine that a whole nation was required to hinge their entire future and well-being on a promise from God. From our perspective, we read this story and think to ourselves, *It's simple; just believe in the promise that God gave you.*

A friend of mine was telling me a story once about a time when she was scuba diving in the ocean. She mentioned that in order not to get lost or disoriented while under the water for extended periods of time, divers want to set their compass to know where the boat is. If they fail to do this, then they will lose their sense of direction and end up lost at sea. This particular time she had forgotten to set her compass to where the boat was, and she was down for a while. At some point, she realized she was lost. So she had to swim back up to the surface to find the boat.

When scuba divers are lost, they have to go back to the surface of the water and look for the boat so they can reorient themselves and reset their compass. This whole process of coming back to the surface is a sign that they messed up, and those on the boat call such divers "prairie dogs," which refers to the prairie dogs in the vast, open fields that pop out of the ground to see what is going on.

Sometimes in our pursuit of the Promised Land, different things come along the way that can deter us from what is ours. One of the things that God has given us is His promises. What we do with these promises is a big deal. They're meant to be that compass that we use to help us always know our direction. If we get lost or discouraged in this pursuit of the Promised Land, then we need to be a prairie dog and get reoriented with the boat again. There are times when I am in this place, and I need to go back and read and remember the promises the Lord has spoken to me so my compass always stays on target.

Personally, I keep track of all the prophetic words and promises the Lord has spoken over my life. I have them transcribed into a document that I keep on my iPad and laptop. If it's an mp3 file, then I will have it readily available to listen to when I need to. This is my way of cultivating my awareness of the promises that are over my life. I would highly encourage all of us to become students and to steward the promises and prophetic words over our lives. This will help us stay on course in the face of anything that comes our way.

ENDNOTES

1. *Merriam-Webster's Collegiate Dictionary,* 11th ed., s.v., "fruit."

2. John Maxwell, *The 21 Irrefutable Laws of Leadership* (Nashville, TN: Thomas Nelson, 1998), 48.

MOMENTUM
MOMENTUM
MOMENTUM
MOMENTUM
MOMENTUM

CHAPTER 4

ACCESS THROUGH HONOR

BILL JOHNSON

I have had a love for revival for as long as I can remember. Every time I would read about revivals, it would make my heart burn. It still does. I would weep, cry out to God, pray with great passion, and just plain hope I could live during a time of great outpouring of the Spirit. My prayers were simple: "God, I will pay any price to have more of You. I must have more. Fill me with Your Spirit beyond the measure I have already known." These are the things I prayed for, sometimes waking myself up in the night—not to pray, but because I was actually praying in my sleep.

We have now been living in a wonderful outpouring of the Spirit for 15 years and counting. Presently, I see more in a month than I thought I'd ever be able to see in my lifetime. I am so thankful, but I'm not satisfied. When He gives us more, He lets us see even more than what we have. He does this to draw us into the place of hunger that we might bring into our day what was reserved for another day.[1]

[handwritten margin note: There is never ~~enough~~ days that can be with & feel His Spirit in the tent all time like Moses Joshua did.]

One of the tools He has used to stir up this hunger in me is reading the record of the great revivals of the past. While it's not always healthy to make comparisons, it is good to learn where God has set a "legal precedent," implying He's likely to do it again. The very nature of a testimony carries with it a revelation of what God wants to do again. It works. I burn when I read the stories of Finney, McPherson, Edwards, Wesley, and others. No effort is required on my part. Such burning is as natural as is breathing. I was born for this.

HOUSE OF GENERALS

The Lord began to speak to me about those who had gone before me, who had often been maligned, misunderstood, persecuted, and opposed. These revivalists paid a price for the people of their day to have a significant encounter with God. My grandfather sat under Smith Wigglesworth's ministry. He once told me, "Not everyone loved Wigglesworth." Of course we love him today. He's dead. Israel loved all their dead prophets, too.

These heroes of the faith made sobering choices to follow God, no matter what. In doing so, they have made it possible for me to have access to things I'd never have access to on my own. The Lord spoke to me about these revivalists, saying, "If you will honor the generals of the past, even those whose lives ended poorly, I will give you access to their anointings." This was a word to our church family, not just to me. Then I remembered that Solomon's life didn't end so well. He started well. But his forbidden marriages brought idolatry into Israel that took 300 years to get rid of. Yet God was not ashamed to note the failure along with the record of his victories and triumphs in Scripture (see 1 Kings 11:4). Hezekiah is one of the greatest revivalists in Scripture. Yet his ending is quite sad and disappointing. But God made sure the record of his obedience is included in the Scriptures that contain the honest record of his disobedience (see 2 Chron. 32:25-33). The Lord then spoke to me about building a revivalist library and museum. It is to be called "The House of Generals."

In response to the command and opportunity, I began to buy revivalist materials whenever I could. My collection had grown significantly, but was still a long way from becoming an actual library. Then Roberts Liardon called one day and made his amazing library and museum available to me for purchase. He had spent decades saving some of the most priceless materials for his collection. Our passions are similar. He had great patience with us in the long process needed for us to actually make the purchase. He did so with a great conviction that we were to have these materials to help to raise up a generation of revivalists who could impact the course of world history. We said yes and made the purchase.

We now have the materials in hand and are looking for the ability to build the actual facility to house these extraordinary materials. But that's another story. More important for this context is that we burn with the conviction that we must give honor to those who have gone before us, regardless of how they ended. We celebrate their victories and learn from their failures.

HONOR THE DISHONORABLE?

Tragically, if I mention the names of certain individuals who were used in history, I am attacked by fellow believers who have no place in their hearts for God using somebody who had problems, even though the Scriptures are filled with such stories.

John Alexander Dowie was an amazing man. He is considered by many to be the father of the healing movement. He was actually jailed 100 times in one year for the Gospel. But he ended poorly. And many would rather pretend that he either never existed or that he was a heretic. It just seems easier to conclude that his ministry was not genuine than it is to admit that God uses imperfect people.

William Branham was an extremely humble man with a most unusual gift in miracles. If ever a man was anointed specifically for the miracle realm, it was he. The stories of trusted men and women of God of his day who watched the Spirit of God come upon this man are to be taken seriously. It is very possible that no one since Jesus Himself carried this particular measure of anointing. But he was not without faults. The strangeness of his doctrine later in life has caused many to once again "throw out the baby with the bath-water." It seems easier to reject a person for error than it is to learn to eat the meat and throw out the bones. One response only needs an opinion; the other requires maturity.

Lonnie Frisbee was the eccentric young man used of God to powerfully impact Calvary Chapel and the Vineyard during the days of the Jesus People Movement. Once again the miracle anointing was extraordinary. He even had the attention and favor of such notables as Kathryn Kuhlman. His Mother's Day service at John Wimber's church in Yorba Linda is a reference point for many. While God had been moving powerfully through the Vineyard for quite some time, Lonnie's unusual gift brought breakthrough at a higher level. He had unusual favor with God. Yet he had great failure in his life. As a result, he died of AIDS. Many skip past his place of influence on our present day. Some will not use his name and will mention him only as an unusual young man. And then others simply ignore his role altogether. God didn't skip such things and doesn't seem to be quite as troubled as we are when someone's sin is so embarrassing.

The names of both victors and failures are many. I use these three only because they came to mind. It's hard to read their stories and not be thankful for the place that they filled in Church history. We didn't choose these people. God did. And while He never gave the stamp of approval to any of the sin issues in their lives, He did use them, knowing of their weaknesses. Why this surprises us is hard for me to understand, considering that none of us are perfect. God doesn't approve of any of our sins or weaknesses. Yet He gives us access to realms of the Spirit to forever set us free.

The failure to take advantage of the grace made available is not the fault of the Gospel, the style of the preachers, the message, or the day they lived in. It is theirs alone. Yet God is not ashamed to let His name be associated with such people. He actually recorded for all to see that His only Son would be born through the lineage of deceivers, liars, adulterers, and even a prostitute. We should be thankful. It means that we, too, qualify for grace and are available to be used by God. But be forewarned. He expects us to take advantage of the grace made available to truly become free. Sin is inexcusable.

Of all people, we should be the most accommodating to those whose lives ended poorly. God uses imperfect people, not as a testimony of His approval of their lives, but to confirm His word preached by those people. We must adjust to His values or else we become dangerously close to dishonoring His work in those who have gone before us. And since there is no one alive to defend them, God will. I personally think that many have gone into spiritual poverty simply because of their careless comments and slander of those who have filled an important place in history. Such careless accusations are not acceptable, even though the person is dead.

We must guard ourselves. If I am careless to criticize, I have opened myself up to the same spirit that deceived them. Is that not what was meant in First Corinthians 10:12: *"Therefore let him who thinks he stands take heed that he does not fall"* (NASB)? The arrogance needed to criticize another is the same arrogance that brings about our own failure. Once again, being "poor in spirit," having total dependency on grace, comes into play. It will save us from much heartache.

"OH NO, NOT THEM!"

I have watched a phenomenon in the things of God. He often puts the very area of spiritual breakthrough we long for most in the camp of believers we least want to be associated with. It really tests our hunger for more. It is the ultimate test to our prayers that say we'll pay any price for revival. Considering the value that God places on humility, it shouldn't surprise us that God would require that of us. After all, Jesus was numbered with two thieves on the cross in His payment for our redemption. In His case, it was humiliating. In ours, we have to learn to associate with believers whose lives, for whatever reason, bring embarrassment to us. As goes the master, so goes the servant.

All of these people, successes and failures, left an inheritance from their victories. The Holy Spirit will give us the wisdom needed to **not** repeat their failures. (Roberts Liardon's book, *God's Generals, Volume 1,*) is required reading in our school for this reason. He points to the weaknesses without bringing undue shame and mockery to their lives.

HONOR MADE PRACTICAL

If any of those I've mentioned were alive today, I'd try to do something to honor them. As it is, I am left to preserve the memory of what they accomplished in God. When I meet a family member of theirs, *I honor them and thank them for their heritage.* I also have them pray for me whenever possible. Several years ago, I met the granddaughter of a great revivalist who had died within the previous decade. She was 12. *I asked her if she would please pray for me*, knowing that she carried a family anointing that could be imparted. Both she and her friend prayed a powerful, but childlike prayer that really impacted me. I was so grateful for the chance to receive something in prayer that was never made available to me in person from the revivalist. In some ways, it was as though I had the man himself standing before me, praying a great prayer of impartation.[2]

We must *stop the slander and the criticisms*, even if the details are true. These people should be held in respect for what they did accomplish for God. The Kingdom culture celebrates people for who they are without stumbling over who they are not. Such is the culture of Heaven. *Refuse to participate in the careless conversations* of other believers who take pleasure in giving such critiques. Nothing significant is ever accomplished through such babble.

I love to study the life of Solomon. His choice for wisdom above wealth, power, and health is legendary. It speaks volumes to me and has done so for years. But he ended poorly. I refuse to criticize him—though I don't refuse to acknowledge his sin, nor do I refuse to set up guards in my own life to learn from his mistakes. It is a complete waste of time to repeat someone else's failure. *Learning from history is needed so we don't repeat the failures of history.* This is a posture we must take: stop slandering the saints of the past. It will only hurt us in our pursuit of more for our lifetime.

We must read their accomplishments, not from the writings of the "dime a dozen" critics, but from the writings of those who have studied their lives without the personal need to tear someone down. As we read, we must let the stories of their breakthroughs become our own by crying out to God. We can lean into their testimonies, knowing that God is no respecter of persons, but is the same yesterday, today, and forever. When we have the conviction that God is willing and ready to do it again, we can *lift up our voices with a fresh hunger* for more. It's hard for me to read the stories of how God used these men and women of God without weeping and crying out to God for more. Let's let the ashes of their lives become the coals for our own. I really believe God values this approach when we actually value those He chose to rest upon.

And finally, we must learn to *honor the Holy Spirit* who rested upon them. Even more specifically, we must give honor to the particular kind of anointing they carried. For example, I am told that William Branham had over 10,000 open visions with 100 percent accuracy in his miracle ministry. This means I must give a place of great value in my heart for this kind of ministry if I want to experience it myself. This usually starts by valuing God's anointing on others who operate in word of knowledge, specifically through open visions. We must refuse the temptation to compare and critique. Rather, we celebrate. For what we celebrate we will be much more likely to participate in.

My LORD, I know I am full of sins, and I do not yet have the faith that Your prophets did. But my Father, one desire in my heart is to hear You in direct words (instead of visions) Your voice and to see You and feel Your true Father, I so much want to be **CONCLUSION** with You, not the blessings or help You can /will give me. Father, I know I'm too sinful to see Your face, but my heart cannot be filled unless I can hear You & be You the way Moses & Enoch were accepted by You.

Honor comes from the heart. Getting rid of the "religious" need to tear others down in order to feel better about ourselves will go a long way in helping us tap into spiritual inheritance. What people have accomplished in the generations before us was always meant to be left for us as an inheritance. But when those lives had poor endings, the Church often feels more justified in also rejecting their ministries, which usually brought about controversy and conflict.

I live the opposite. It seems to me that if the devil is going to work that hard to destroy certain individuals' impact on future generations, then maybe I should pay extra attention to their ministries. After all, counterfeiters never counterfeit pennies. They're not worth the effort. They only counterfeit things of great value, like one hundred-dollar bills. If the devil works to destroy or counterfeit someone's anointed ministry, then he affirms its value. That means we approach their realm of ministry with hunger, caution, and family. It is in the context of accountability and corporate pursuit (family) that we can experience breakthrough and success where others have failed.

ENDNOTES

1. For a more complete study on this concept, see Chapter 10, "Pulling Tomorrow Into Today," in my book *Dreaming With God*.

2. For the best teaching I've ever seen on this subject, get Randy Clark's book, *There's More*. He brings much needed understanding to a beautiful part of the Gospel, one that is vital to the subject of spiritual inheritance.

MOMENTUM
MOMENTUM
MOMENTUM
MOMENTUM
MOMENTUM

CHAPTER 5

FOREVER AND EVER

I will make you a great nation; I will bless you and make your name great; and you shall be a blessing. I will bless those who bless you, and I will curse him who curses you; and in you all the families of the earth shall be blessed (Genesis 12:2-3).

CONFRONTING MINDSETS
THAT CONTRADICT LIFE

We tend to never question bad news. Whenever we hear or read about some bad news, we usually don't think, *It can't be that bad,* or *This isn't true.* We usually embrace it as accurate information. However, when we hear good news, we usually have thoughts along the lines of, *It can't be that good,* or *That can't be completely true.* This is a result of a mindset that can't embrace the reality that, in the Kingdom, life is meant to continue.

Unfortunately, our unredeemed mindset has allowed us to accept things that happen to us as what was meant to happen. This allowance creates a standard by which we live and view life. When this takes place, we then create an ecosystem that perpetuates itself. Our beliefs and perspective become jaded in a way that makes us struggle to see the true heart of God in the matter.

Why do we question good news? It's because we have allowed our circumstances to shape us in a way that expects good things to end. In the Kingdom, when life is created, it continues to bring life. Anything outside of the Kingdom teaches us that good things end. So what world do we want to live from? The Kingdom or outside of the Kingdom?

This type of mindset is one that lives *under* the circumstances instead of living *above* the circumstances. It can look like this— instead of us happening to life, life is happening to us. If we are going to be moving into a paradigm that brings continual life everywhere we go, then we must confront this mindset. Now I realize that life does present its ugly side. The point isn't whether or not bad days happen, the point is whether we want to live under them or above them.

The first step in confronting this mindset is learning to recognize when it rears its ugly head. Not when it fully manifests itself, but when it's subtle, for example, when thoughts like these come along: *I'm not sure if I will get healed. I probably won't get that good job. When is this good season going to end? When is the bad day coming?* We can confront this mindset by overriding it with Kingdom reality. When we understand the way the Kingdom works, we begin to make adjustments internally to come into alignment with that reality that will manifest externally.

When I was in junior high, our family decided to have some foster kids live with us for a period of time. Their names were Stephan and Eric. They were placed in our home because the parents had both died. I can clearly remember the very first night they were with us. As we sat at the dinner table, the look on their faces was a mixture of sadness and shock. Here were two young boys at the ages of 6 and 4, having just experienced the horrible tragedy of losing their parents, and now they were sitting in the home of strangers.

After we prayed over our dinner, we served them some food. I remember watching them sit with their arms wrapped around their plates as they inhaled their food with such speed I couldn't help but stare in amazement. They were eating so fast and guarding their plates because they were not used to having food available. Their lives had taught them that when something good comes around, it's best to get it while you can.

In their minds they might not get a good meal for a while, so they ate a lot of it and ate it fast. During dinner, my parents explained to Stephan and Eric that, as long as they were in our house, there would always be food on the table. It took a couple of weeks for them to fully realize that there would always be food on the table. After a while they ate at a normal speed.

When we realize we have access to food all the time, we change the way we act and respond to life. We are no longer driven by fear of lack; we now live in a place of abundance. This is the essence of understanding inheritance as it promotes us spiritually, physically, and emotionally to a level that gives us Kingdom authority.

Many consider the Book of Ephesians to be the best book written by Paul. It was addressed to a church in Ephesus. This is not a normal letter from Paul. This one displays Paul's love and affection to this specific church. After reading this book, we begin to sense the passion that Paul carried for this church to embrace a lifestyle and mindset that would create such life and abundance that it would usher in the Kingdom in greater measure. It gives us access points that will help us to go deeper into the Kingdom.

A lot of believers aren't aware that the very thing hindering them from stepping into a Kingdom lifestyle is the fact that they don't believe they can. So they resort to inaction or striving.

We are taught by our culture to get ready for a bad day or a bad season. So we tend to make adjustments that don't line up with the Kingdom. Sometimes those adjustments stop the flow of life. God is the same yesterday, today, and forever (see Heb. 13:8). This is the very thing that we must line everything else up with—not just in theory, but in reality. The more we understand the Kingdom, the more we will begin to position ourselves for a constant flow of life.

Electrical power grids consist of a mass network of cables, wiring, power stations, and substations that point to a little socket in the wall. The power is always on; it's constant. The issue isn't if the power is there; the issue is whether we are plugged into the grid. It's not an issue of whether God is on or not; it's whether we are plugged into the source. The Kingdom is always on and expanding.

As we study the history of revival, we find evidence of a certain repetition. Wherever moves of God take place, people's lives are transformed, cities and nations are changed, and people are touched by God. Miracles and healings take place, marriages are restored, and businesses prosper. Then the revival seems to die out as the generation that it started in begins to pass away.

The word *revival* actually means "restoration of life." It's a word we typically use for a move of God of some capacity. Revival happens when something that once was dead now becomes infused with life. For many, the word *revival* is synonymous with church meetings in which the power of God shows up and people surrender themselves to Jesus and get healed of various levels of sickness and disease. One of our hobbies is to read the old revival stories, and we can't help but get excited and begin to set our hearts toward it happening again.

Let me pose a couple of questions. Does the Kingdom need revival? Did Jesus need revival? If the Kingdom is meant to create life and continues to create life, then is revival necessary? I am suggesting that it is possible for us never to need personal revival because we never lost life in the first place. There are times and seasons when this infusion of life is heightened, but, in general, there is a flow of life. As the Body of Christ, we need to carry the mindset that when God creates something, it also is meant to continue to create life.

You can look into history and see moves of God that ended because of people's decisions. This is the effect of not co-laboring with God. When we co-labor with Him, things begin to multiply and generate momentum. When we stop co-laboring with Him, we are usually at the beginning of the end.

SALVATION IS BIGGER THAN WE THINK

If we can begin to equip a generation with an understanding of what they have access to by inheritance, we will see things take place that have not yet been seen. Instead of being a people who wait for their time to end, they will begin to live a life that has only begun.

Jesus said, *"Do not fear, little flock, for it is your Father's good pleasure to give you the kingdom"* (Luke 12:32).

These types of phrases echoed out of the mouth of Jesus and began to set in motion a force that would ultimately turn the world upside down time and time again. The ministry of Jesus had one supreme focus: on earth as it is in Heaven. For the 33 years of His life, He demonstrated this through His actions, words, and lifestyle. This can be seen in His feeding of the 5,000 (see Matt. 14:13-21); the opening of blind eyes (see Matt. 9:27-31); the revelation of the new covenant (see Matt. 26:28); the raising of the dead (see John 11:38-44)—and the list goes on.

The nature of the Kingdom is set up so that when life is created, it continues to create life. Genesis begins the story of creation, the detailed account of how God created the world and the universe that we live in. When God spoke, it happened. Another way to look at it is that when God spoke, His words created life, and not only that, but they set something in motion that hasn't stopped. Creation as we know it has been reproducing, adjusting, and expanding since it was first spoken into existence. During creation, He said, *"Let there be light"* (Gen. 1:3), and it's still working! This truth intrigues me immensely. It is evident that God is in the business of sustainment.

The key is for us to understand this momentum and eventually learn our role in the process. The Church as a whole largely has missed this principle. We have mastered the art of enjoying life when it's in front of us. But we haven't moved into a position of stewarding that life to a place of inheritance and increase. We are moving into a new realm that will give us a new level of understanding: When life is created, we will know how to step into our place to help facilitate more life.

Now the LORD had said to Abram: "Get out of your country, from your family and from your father's house, to a land that I will show you. I will make you a great nation; I will bless you and make your name great; and

you shall be a blessing. I will bless those who bless you,
and I will curse him who curses you; and in you all the
families of the earth shall be blessed" (Genesis 12:1-3).

God's promise echoed this very principle of continual life. God declared to Abram, *"I will make you a great nation,"* and *"in you all the families of the earth will be blessed."* What was God doing? He was displaying His nature by separating Abram from an idolatrous family to establish a family that was patterned after His idea of a family. God's idea of family is one that is blessed and walks in favor. God has a plan to make people jealous for Him. Notice how His promise to Abram was not limited to one family; He promised that Abram was going to be a father to the nations and that all families would be blessed.

Apart from Adam and Eve, this is one of the earliest examples of how God intended to establish Himself with us and create a foundation for His Kingdom to come. It was on the basis of family. This is a really important Kingdom concept to understand. It is this concept that the enemy has worked hard to twist. In our day, a lot of people's experience of family is dysfunctional, disempowering, and, ultimately, no fun to be around. Those family problems have caused generations of people to become, independent apart from family. Independence in the context of family is healthy, but once we take independence out of that context, then we stop or step out of momentum.

One of the things God is doing in our time is restoring families and relationships. I see more people going after the restoration of relationships with family and friends than I have seen before. This is really encouraging as it's an early sign of a generation of people stepping into the flow of blessing that was promised to Abraham.

God intends His people to become great. He then reaffirms this by saying He will bless anyone who blesses them and curse anyone who curses them. God distinguishes His nature by saying, "I am creating something with you and in you. Then anyone can have access to it." There is a momentum in place, and we can step into or step out of it.

In the Old Testament, when God blesses a nation, many times you will see other nations come and ask, "What must I do to get what you have?" It's God's ultimate marketing strategy: We become jealous for who He is.

In Psalm 67:1-2, we read,

> *God be merciful to us and bless us, and cause His face to shine upon us, that Your way may be known on earth, Your salvation among all nations.*

The writer knew that when God's favor is upon the people, the supernatural will naturally happen, and His Kingdom will be established on earth: *"Then the earth shall yield her increase; God, our own God, shall bless us"* (Ps. 67:6). I can't help but think what it will be like when we believers step into this reality of God's face shining upon us; one of the results will be the earth responding by "yielding her increase." Now what happens in the spiritual will manifest in the natural.

In establishing Abraham as a father of nations, God was painting a picture for history to see that He is the bringer and creator of life and that life flows from Him. He can't help but emanate life. The question is, will we let God establish us to walk in the blessing and favor that brings life wherever we go?

Another great example of this principle of continual life is found in the life and heritage of King David. Many of us know

David as a worshiper and lover of God, a songwriter, a warrior, a murderer, and an adulterer. He has quite a resumé. But we tend to overlook something that I believe is just as powerful, if not more. And that is the heritage and legacy he left for the generations to come. The decisions that King David made in his lifetime created a flow of life that lasted longer than his life.

> *And he walked in the way of the kings of Israel, just as the house of Ahab had done, for the daughter of Ahab was his wife; and he did evil in the sight of the LORD. Yet the LORD would not destroy Judah, **for the sake of his servant David, as He promised him to give a lamp to him and his sons forever*** (2 Kings 8:18-19).

> *May the guilt of their blood rest on the head of Joab and his descendants forever. But on David and his descendants, his house and his throne, may there be the **LORD's peace forever*** (1 Kings 2:33 NIV).

> *But King Solomon will be blessed, and David's throne will remain secure before the **LORD forever*** (1 Kings 2:45 NIV).

In looking at David's life, I want to address several things that will help us understand how the "Lord's peace" remained on his house forever. The first step is to understand David as a worshiper. From a young age, David was often found singing to God in pure worship and adoration when no one else was looking. He was a true worshiper before he ever became known. As we look at his life, we can see his pure passion for worship. David was absolutely caught up more by who God is than by what God does.

Any time we are more consumed by what God does than who He is, we begin to miss the point of what He does. The act of worship is never about us and what He does for us. It's all about who He is. If we begin to approach the act of worship because of what He does, we then fall into the trap of trying to manipulate Him to do what we want with our worship.

Let's look at a practical example. People tend to flock to wealthy people because they have something they need. People will often act differently and treat them differently. They change into something they are not in hopes of gaining something from these wealthy people. They attempt to manipulate wealthy people by how they treat them and act around them. It's a shallow form of worship, and it's called flattery.

One time one of my daughters was sick with a fever, and I remember walking into her room late at night to check on her. When I checked on her, I could see she was still sick, and her fever was still high. As I stood looking over her, I had this thought that if I worshiped God right then, maybe He would come and heal her. So I began to worship Him quietly since my daughter was sleeping. Instantly a conviction came over me, and I realized that I had moved into a position to "get" God to do something because I was worshiping Him. What a horrible revelation. I was attempting to manipulate God by what I was doing. Immediately, I repented for trying to flatter God with my worship.

There is nothing wrong with admiring what God does. In fact, we are instructed to be expert stewards of what God does and to always remember His goodness and works. So desiring what He does is not an issue. But it can become an issue when admiring what He does doesn't lead us to worship who He is. It's important that our pursuit of supernatural signs and wonders leads us to the destination of who God is.

So when we worship God in spirit and in truth, it is beautiful and perfect. David's life of worship created in him a heart that was after God, and God loved it. Pure and perfect worship is selfless. It has no agenda, no strings attached, no motive—just a desire to give Him what we have to give.

GRACE HURTS SO GOOD

On a certain day many years ago, two unseen forces collided as a result of one man's decision. This day was fashioned in the heart of God from days of old. A force was at work that was putting a limit on what humankind could accomplish. This limit was much like a governor on an engine. The governor on an engine is designed to allow only a certain amount of fuel into the motor, which limits the true strength of the motor. This unseen force was a governor for humankind; it put a limit on people's capacity to do things. However, that was about to change when this one man, Jesus, decided to do the unthinkable—to pay the price for us to have life beyond what people were even capable of imagining.

This unseen force that limited humankind can be summed up in these words: *the Law*. The Law was designed to show people what was required of them outside of relationship with God. When we can't live in relationship, then the Law is a default to show us how to live our lives. But as we found out over time, it was impossible to uphold the Law. Instead of moving away from the Law and moving into relationship with God, people decided to work even harder at keeping the Law, which led many to be enslaved by something so lifeless.

Leaders of the day began to set even more strict requirements to uphold, which made it literally impossible to be successful. More and more people began to almost unintentionally abandon the path of life and choose the path of death.

The Law had entrenched many into a lifestyle of slavery to a list of words, and it gave them no hope of freedom. It wreaked havoc on people's ability to see God as loving. The paradigm was bent on an angry God. Fear became the lens and filter through which people lived their lives. Every move was made with fear in mind. People became extremely powerless. This reduced their ability to make moral decisions that brought life. It also reduced their ability to live in relationship. Instead, it brought destruction. It could be seen in families, schools, marketplace, and everyday life.

When Jesus reached the age of 33, the "unthinkable" plan was beginning to unfold. This decision to sacrifice His life so we could live was more than just a means to getting to Heaven; it gave us access to a realm of righteousness and life that was only possible through relationship with God. Jesus then introduced us to an even greater unseen force called *grace*.

Something violent took place on the day of the crucifixion. It was clearly the opposite of a peaceful day—not just in the fact that Jesus had been brutally murdered to the pleasing of the crowd, but because behind it all something huge was taking place. One force called the Law was being overthrown by a greater force called grace. This would ultimately alter the course of history.

For many, our understanding of grace is that it is the one thing that is going to keep us out of hell and get us to Heaven. And that is true. However, my concern is that we have reduced it to *just* that.

Grace has no limit or end. We can't find the boundaries of grace. *"Of the increase of His government and peace, there will be no end..."* (Isa. 9:7). Isaiah was prophesying about a time when God will turn things around completely. He was foretelling of when Jesus would live a life and ultimately pay the price for something that would have "no end," which means that the end does not exist.

Paul makes a really powerful statement in Galatians 1:8: *"But even if we, or an angel from heaven, preach any other gospel to you than what we have preached to you, let him be accursed."* What's he saying? He is letting the churches in the region of Galatia know not to allow any other Gospel or teaching to come in and take them away from what Paul had taught them in the beginning. And if he or an angel came and told them something different, they had the right to curse him and completely disregard what he said. What was the original Gospel that Paul was referring to? It was the message of grace.

When people receive Christ, such a level of freedom and joy comes over them, which is so much fun to see and be part of. But more often than not, they eventually step away from what was given to them for free and start trying to earn it. Most of the time, it's done unknowingly, yet the freedom and joy begin to fade away. Was this the plan of God? Was grace given so we could become guiltier? When we allow grace to make us guiltier, we then move back under the Law and out of relationship with God.

Our identity will reveal our ability to embrace grace. We have all had times in life when things were going really well and times when things were going horribly wrong. If someone asked us if our character was tested in those times when things weren't going well, the majority of us would easily reply yes—which is true. Some of my lowest moments in life have been when I found out who I really was, and I became stronger as a result of that. I can also say that in my highest moments in life, I found out even more about who I am.

Someone once said, "Give a man power, and it will test his character." When people have more than their needs require, another part of their character will be revealed. What we don't realize is that what we do the moment we get things that we dreamed of and hoped for also reveals much about us.

If you were $10,000 in debt and someone came up to you and said, "Here is $10,000, and I want to give it to you," you would take the money and be so happy that you were no longer in debt. That money enabled you to get out of debt and move into a break-even point. Now, if some time later someone else came up to you and said the same thing, "Here is $10,000, and I want to give it to you," your response would most likely be to take the money and be thankful that you could now live in abundance. Let's say this continued—every day, someone wanted to give you $10,000. At some point, it would be uncomfortable, awkward, and too much to handle. You would then find a way to turn it down because you "have enough."

When we're in need, it's easier to receive a gift. So when our need is met and our hole is filled, we will begin to see how we respond to abundance. At times we don't necessarily have glaring needs. In those moments, we tend to neglect the free gift. For some, this would bring them to a place of eventually saying, "Please, you have already given me enough, and you don't need to give me any more." So they'd look for ways to neglect it. For others, they might start feeling obligated, and they would feel like they needed to earn this money because it couldn't be possible that they could keep receiving it for free.

This can happen in our salvation. This is why I believe many people don't fully understand the fullness of salvation. It has often been reduced to just being saved from going to hell because of our sins. With this incomplete understanding of salvation, people realize their sins are forgiven. In other words, their debt has been paid, and they are now at break-even point. Then the attitude shifts to trying to earn the rest of their salvation. This takes people outside of the intent of grace, which is designed to take them into a realm of abundance in all areas of life.

What we fail to realize is that we turn off the faucet that was meant to give us life. In order to be a river, we have to have a constant flow of fresh water. The apostle Paul addresses this throughout his books. If we continue to neglect the free gift of grace and attempt to earn it, we will become a swamp. A swamp is a body of water that doesn't get an influx of fresh water; after awhile it gets stale and begins to produce things that live on decay.

Francis Frangipane puts it this way:

> Every area in your thinking that glistens with hope in God is an area which is being liberated by Christ. But any system of thinking that does not have hope, which feels hopeless, is a stronghold which must be pulled down.[1]

We are designed to be a river of continual life. When we became believers, we were then ushered into a constant flow of life. It is our responsibility to stay in that place.

But whoever drinks of the water that I shall give him will never thirst. But the water that I shall give him will become in him a fountain of water springing up into everlasting life (John 4:14).

Nowhere in the Bible does it say, "When you've had enough, you can turn it off." In fact, it says to keep asking for more (see Zech. 10:1). In the parable of the talents, the one guy who didn't do anything with his one talent had it taken from him and given to the guy who had the most (see Matt. 25:14-30). This is a different concept than we are used to. We think that's only for when we don't have anything. Just when we think we have enough, God starts saying, "You can't even begin to scratch the surface of what I have for you."

COFFEE

A number of years ago, I was reading my Bible one night before going to bed. As I was reading, I felt the Lord tell me, "I'm going to take you to the mountaintop to teach you something." For the next 18 months, I had a unique and fun experience, and it had to do with coffee, which is one of the finer things in life.

It started out one night in the drive-thru at Starbucks. I had placed my order for a cup of pure black goodness—coffee. When I pulled up to the window, the guy handed me my drink and said, "The car in front of you paid for your drink." I thought, "That's nice." The very next week, I was in the same drive-thru waiting for my cup of pure goodness, but this time the line was taking an abnormally long time. Now we all know 10 seconds in a drive-thru line is more like an hour. Finally, I got to the window to receive my drink, but this time the guy in the window said, "Sir, we are so sorry. We had an accident in here tonight, so this drink is on the house tonight." So now two visits in a row, I didn't have to pay for my cup of coffee. This went on for <u>18 months.</u> It was extremely hard for me to purchase a cup of coffee or to buy a bag of coffee.

Another time, I was having a quick, 15-minute meeting with a staff member at the church. Since it was a quick meeting, we met in the stairway at the end of a long hallway. At the opposite end of the hallway from us was our *HeBrews* coffee shop. As we were meeting, I was thinking to myself, *I would really like a cup of coffee.* I had planned that after this little meeting, I would walk down to *HeBrews* to get a cup. As these thoughts filled my head, a gentleman walked up to us with a cup of coffee in hand and said, "I have no idea why I bought this cup of coffee; I don't even drink coffee. Would one of you want this?" I quickly looked over to the guy I was meeting with, and he didn't want it, so I gladly received the cup of coffee. This is what revival must look like: we have a thought, and it happens.

As these 18 months began to unfold, it exposed something in me: the part of my identity that neglected something when I have had enough of it. This experience taught me to learn how to receive beyond my comfort levels—that I don't have permission to stop something when I've had enough. So every time I take a sip of a cup of coffee, it's a great reminder of this important lesson in living in <u>abundance</u> with the King.

[handwritten margin note: t feel "guilty" receiving any our God, even 's not our "need."]

When we begin to move into a new understanding of abundance, it's typical to start having thoughts like, *I don't deserve this,* or *Why me?* We're right, but this abundance is not hinging on that. It's hinging on the fact that He is so extravagant and that we don't have a right to turn down or turn off the abundance once it's on. Most people position themselves in a way that when they get to a certain point of being a "good" person, then they are ready to receive from God. What we can't forget is that it's His goodness that leads us to repentance (see Rom. 2:4). We tend to reverse that verse and live our lives thinking that repentance leads us to His goodness. God designed it so that He would unleash His goodness on us, and that would then reveal our need to repent and change the way we think. It was never about what we could do.

If we expect to be entrusted with His goodness, then we must learn not to reject it. Sometimes this abundance and favor hurts. I have been in a time in life where I am so surrounded by favor that it has made me really insecure at times. It has humbled me beyond previous experience. What I am learning in all this is that I am responsible to keep myself positioned under it. It's illegal for me to step out of it because I can't handle it.

This is what Paul was saying: Don't let any other teaching remove you from this favor and grace that I told you about because it's human nature to "repent" to get more of His goodness. If that were the case, then grace would be based on our ability—and then we could have a boasting contest of what we can do.

If we expect to do what's humanly impossible, then this is a key for doing just that. But if we choose to live under the lie that His goodness is based on what we can do, then we have reduced ourselves to what is humanly possible. If we embrace grace, we will defy all logic and reason, the realm of physics and the parameters of reality, and do what is humanly impossible.

In his epistles, Paul used some phrases that give us a peek into the revelation that he walked in regarding this Gospel of grace. The phrases are *beggarly elements* and *basic principles* (see Gal. 4:9; Col. 2:8). Paul made a strong argument that we are not subject to the religious and world system.

Something took place when Jesus was walking on water (see Matt. 14:25). Not only was He doing something simply amazing, but He was displaying something that we have access to. Jesus was demonstrating that there is a realm of authority that will enable us to defy the natural laws of the universe. Not only did He defy the logic and reason of the human mind, but He displayed the possibility of living in a realm where the "elements" of this world are inferior to Kingdom authority.

I have a strong conviction that there is a day coming when the Body of believers will be so actively released into a realm of authority that it will stun the courts of Heaven. I can't help but think of what Jesus was implying when He said, "You will do far greater things than I ever did" (see John 14:12). That is a pretty astounding statement considering what Jesus did in His lifetime. Now let's embrace our place in grace!

ENDNOTE

1. Francis Frangipane, *The Three Battlegrounds* (Cedar Rapids, IA: Arrow Publications, 1989), 39.

CHAPTER 6

INHERITING THE SUPERNATURAL

BILL JOHNSON

> This chapter is reprinted from my book, *The Supernatural Power of the Transformed Mind*. While there is some overlap in content, we felt it was important enough to include in this book.

We have inherited every spiritual blessing in Christ. He wants us to discover the "spending power" of our inheritance!

I t's the Lord's desire that the supernatural territory we occupy, the realms of life where we consistently demonstrate His authority, grow larger and more powerful as we pass it on to the next generation. Inheritance is a biblical concept. Proverbs says, *"Houses and riches are an inheritance from fathers..."* (Prov. 19:14). Deuteronomy 29:29 says,

The secret things belong to the LORD our God, but those things which are revealed belong to us and to our chil- dren forever, that we may do all the words of this law.

What is the purpose of a natural inheritance? To give children a leg up so they don't have to start where their parents started. So they don't have to save for ten years to buy a house or start a business. Those who are blessed enough to leave something significant to their children give them a head start, with the hope that they will go farther, faster during their lifetimes. It's simply not true that everyone has to start at the same point and go through the same hardships. It's a biblical concept that one generation would provide a boost for the next. but we are not judged by God by our position through inheritance

A spiritual inheritance works the same way. It enables the next generation to start where the previous generation left off. It's the intent of the Lord for us to wake up to this, one of the most significant yet overlooked principles in the Christian life. He wants generations to pass on their spiritual inheritances. You see, with an inheritance, we get for free what someone else paid for. Sometimes we inherit graces from the Lord where we don't have to go through some of the processes a previous generation went through. That doesn't fit the do-it-yourself motto of the age, but it's the way it works with God. It's like when a person lays hands on other people to impart a grace for a certain area of life and ministry. Those people get the grace for free. That's the way things work in the Kingdom. We see somebody who has a great anointing in healing and we ask them to pray for us, and from that point on, we begin to pray for people, and we see things happen that we never saw happen before. That's an inheritance.

A spiritual inheritance is about making us more effective and efficient in our representation of the King and His Kingdom. It is not for our gratification. It's delightful, it's enjoyable, it's pleasant, it's encouraging, but it's not simply for personal consumption. It is to open doors so that the King and His Kingdom have influence in more places than before.

A spiritual inheritance differs from a natural inheritance in one key way: A natural inheritance gives us something we did not have before. But a spiritual inheritance pulls back the curtain and reveals what we already have permission to possess. That's why it says, *"...But those things which are revealed belong to us and to our children forever..."* (Deut. 29:29).

What's needed is simply the awareness of what is already there. Receiving a spiritual inheritance is like learning that years ago somebody put ten million dollars in your bank account. You had the money all along, but now you are at liberty to spend it, because you have knowledge that the money is there and belongs to you. This is what Paul was trying to get across when he wrote,

> *Therefore let no one boast in men. For all things are yours: whether Paul or Apollos or Cephas, or the world or life or death, or things present or things to come— all are yours. And you are Christ's, and Christ is God's* (1 Corinthians 3:21-23).

> *He who did not spare His own Son, but delivered Him up for us all, how shall He not with Him also freely give us all things?* (Romans 8:32)

> *But as it is written: "Eye has not seen, nor ear heard, nor have entered into the heart of man the things which God has prepared for those who love Him." But God*

has revealed them to us through His Spirit....Now we have received, not the spirit of the world, but the Spirit who is from God, that we might know the things that have been freely given to us by God (1 Corinthians 2:9-10,12).

When we learn of our inheritance, suddenly we have "spending power" with God. We call on resources we didn't know about before. When a previous generation passes on a spiritual inheritance, they pass on all the knowledge and experience they gained in a certain spiritual area.

TRAGEDY OF THE AGES...

But through two thousand years of revival history, no generation has ever passed its revival to the next generation effectively. No generation has raised up the next to carry the momentum of a great outpouring of the Spirit and then had them take it to the next level. Time and again the ball gets dropped. The spiritual territory that was once occupied becomes unoccupied, and the enemy comes to repossess familiar turf. After some time, another generation rises up, having become discontent, and begins to re-dig the wells of revival. But they start at about the same place as before. The well got filled with earth, symbolizing humanity, which is made of earth. We suffer setback after setback from generation to generation, and what should be a point of passing the baton becomes a place of starting over.

The last two thousand years of history show us that a revival will come and last two to four years, then fade out. Because of this pattern, an entire branch of theology has developed that says revival is supposed to arrive periodically to give the Church a shot in the arm—new enthusiasm, new hunger, new energy. But by saying that revival is an exception, a pit stop for refueling, normal Christianity is defined way down. I say rather that revival is not the exception; revival is normal. Signs, wonders, and miracles are as normal to the Gospel as it is normal for you to get up in the morning and breathe. Revival *is* the Christian life; we can't dissect the two. We were never intended to live a season of life outside of the outpouring of the Spirit of God. He always takes us *"from glory to glory"* (see 2 Cor. 3:18). He is progressive in every move He makes. The nature of His Kingdom is that *"Of the increase of His government and peace there will be no end…"* (Isa. 9:7).

The tragedy of history is that revival comes and goes, and subsequent generations build monuments around the achievements of the previous generation, but do not completely receive and occupy their inherited spiritual territory. Perhaps they don't want to pay the same price their forefathers paid, or perhaps they end up forming organizations around past movements to preserve and defend the idea, but not the practice, of revival. In either case, they inherit territory for free, but do not pay the price to develop it, and so they lose it. You see, it's possible to live in inherited territory for a time without advancing that territory. But if we want to hold onto that territory, we must expand it, and to expand it, we will have to pay a price. The quickest way to lose something is to take a defensive posture where we maintain what we have instead of working to increase it. We learn that in the parable of the talents, where God condemned the man who did not put his money to use, but buried it in the ground. (See Matthew 25:14-29.) To choose not to expand and increase is to choose to lose the very thing we are trying to protect.

This principle is further illustrated in Luke 11:24-26 where Jesus said,

> *When an unclean spirit goes out of a man, he goes through dry places, seeking rest; and finding none, he says, "I will return to my house from which I came." And when he comes, he finds it swept and put in order. Then he goes and takes with him seven other spirits more wicked than himself, and they enter and dwell there; and the last state of that man is worse than the first.*

When a person gets set free, there is a moment when he is absolutely clean and purged from filthiness. From that moment on he has the responsibility of managing that liberty. Jesus used a house to illustrate it. The house is clean and swept, there's no furniture, no inhabitants there, but it's newly renovated and beautiful. It's now the owner's responsibility to set up housekeeping, to set up the furniture, to dwell in it, to occupy that home. One of our greatest problems is the failure to occupy the inheritance that we've been given.

Throughout the years, certain individuals broke into new spiritual territory: Smith Wigglesworth, Aimee Semple McPherson, A.B. Simpson, and many other giants of the faith we could name. They didn't start out as giants, but they were possessed by a passion to pursue new territories that had not been occupied before, even when all logic and reason warred against them. They were like people on a safari chopping down undergrowth in the jungle to move into uninhabited territory. They were fed up with seeing one standard in the Bible and another standard in their experience. That discontentment caused them to move dangerously into territory that had been inhabited by violent beasts, if you will (see Exod. 23:29). And so they began to possess territory that had not been possessed by anyone continuously since the days of the apostles. They did it at great personal risk and sacrifice and entered into things that were completely unknown to the Church at that time.

But what was gained by past generations has not been occupied and advanced by those who followed. The house is swept and clean, but because it was not occupied, the enemy came back seven times worse. The word *house* in Scripture can refer to an individual, a family, a local church, a denomination, even to your ministry, gift, and calling. But our country is pockmarked by institutions which once were advancing into unoccupied spiritual territory, and then became reoccupied by the enemy. For example, one of these former hot spots was once a great revival center. For a season it became almost the focal point of the nation. If you wanted to see what God wanted to do on the planet, you could look there. That place was Yale University. When it was established, Yale's goal was not to raise up nice Christian people, but to raise up Holy Ghost revivalists. They paid a price to move into uninhabited territory. But today the school isn't producing revivalists, but anti-Christian secularists. How do you get from revival center to secular stronghold? Gradually, by one generation after another yielding territory instead of embracing their inheritance. Compromise starts when we fail to maintain what we have been given, when we stop moving into new territory, from glory to glory. When they began to compromise in that vital area, they backed up. The territory they once occupied became inhabited by the enemy, and the very thing that was once a strength now became their greatest weakness.

Show me a church or a family whose forefathers broke into significant signs and wonders in the realm of healing, and I can

assure you that if the following generations did not work to maintain and expand that previous standard, they were heavily afflicted
and diseased. When the victories of past generations go unoccupied, they become the platform from which the enemy mocks the
victories of the past generation. Worse yet, that unoccupied territory becomes the military encampment from which the enemy
launches an assault against the people of God to erase from their
memories their inherited victories. When we back off of the standard that God has set, we literally invite the devourer to destroy.
Instead of building on the work of the John G. Lakes, Smith Wig-
glesworths, and Aimee Semple McPhersons, we build memorials
to their memories, and forget what we should have inherited. We
applaud the buildings they were in; we tell the stories of their great
accomplishments. And the place that they occupied is now inhabited by the enemy himself. And so a generation like ours becomes
dissatisfied once again, discontent at seeing a biblical standard and
a lifestyle that falls short. And we once again have to re-dig a well,
remove the humanistic, rationalistic approach to life that denies
the Creator Himself and His involvement—intimate, personal
involvement—in the affairs of man. We get back to the springs of
life and joy.

A few hundred years ago a great revivalist named John Wesley
began to occupy new spiritual territory. But first he came to the
U.S. to be a pastor and had very little success. He boarded a ship
to return to England, and he was depressed. During the journey
they faced some terrible storms, and he feared for his life, but there
was a group of radical believers on board called the Moravians. He
watched them and realized, "We don't know the same Jesus." He
was already a pastor, but as a result of the presence and power of
God on the Moravians, he was truly born again.

He went back to England and became the father of the Meth-odist movement, a group of revivalists and fire-breathing believers. Thousands and thousands would gather in fields to hear Wesley preach. Having meetings outside was totally against convention, but Wesley and George Whitfield broke all the standards of the day. People would climb trees to see Wesley, and he would warn them, "Don't get up in the trees," because the power of God would come and bodies would fall to the ground. God would sweep through those meetings. The Methodists had a slogan: "Organized to beat the devil." They were called "Method-ists" because they created structure, not for structure's sake, but to set the boundaries for God to do something significant in their midst. Their discipling process is legendary. They pastored 100,000 people through this process of raising up leaders who would raise up leaders who would raise up leaders. It's an amazing story.

And yet, within recent days, that very movement ordained a lesbian minister. Let's not misunderstand—Jesus loves lesbians, but He intends to get them out of that lifestyle. The point is, territory broken into by John and Charles Wesley, by John's wife, by those in leadership, and by the many forgotten revivalist preachers, has been lost. Through a lifestyle of risk, they broke into uncharted territory, riding horses from town to town to preach the Gospel. Wesley put a stake down and passed that ground on to the following generation, and they built monuments to his accomplishments as they withdrew from territory he once occupied, trying to make the Gospel more palatable, more understandable. After all, it's not necessary to suffer all that persecution, to have all those bad things said about you. They withdrew, perhaps out of good, reasonable intent, but they left vacated territory behind them, and the very things they were strongest in—great deliverance and freedom from bondage—have become their greatest weakness.

There are many other examples through history, but the point is simple. Every generation of revivalists has been fatherless as it pertains to the move of the Spirit. Every generation has had to learn from scratch how to recognize the Presence, how to move with Him, how to pay a price. The answer to this tragedy is inheritance, where you and I receive something for free. What we do with it determines what happens in the following generations. God is serious about returning for a glorious Church. He's serious that nations should serve Him—not just a token representation from every tribe and tongue, but entire nations, entire people groups apprehended by God Himself.

Can you imagine what would happen if entire nations stepped into the gifts they have from God? Where the song of praise, the declarations of God and His greatness and goodness became visibly manifest on a people? That's His heart. But if we're to get there, we must understand and embrace our spiritual inheritance. We were never intended to start over from scratch every two or three generations. God wants to put each generation at a higher level than the previous one. Every generation has a ceiling experience that becomes the next generation's floor. We dishonor our forefathers and the great price they paid to get their breakthrough by not maintaining and expanding what they accomplished. They attained by taking tremendous risks and persevering under ridicule and rejection. The things we take for granted today cost the previous generation tremendously.

DEFYING THE NATURAL ORDER...

Inheritance helps us to build truth on top of truth. Instead of starting over each generation, we inherit certain truths that allow us to move forward into new areas. For example, when we come to Christ, we become *servants* of the Most High God. Servant-hood is a very strong reality of our relationship with the Lord. But there is a superior truth, and that is *friendship*. Friendship is greater than servanthood. Both are true, and we don't leave servanthood to become a friend, but we build friendship on top of the experience and revelation of servanthood.

That is how we are to move into new territory, by building on precept after precept. Truth is progressive and multi-dimensional. It constantly evolves as we grow, though it never evolves into something that contradicts its foundations. There are measures and levels of anointing that cause the reality of the Scripture to change for us. In fact, a generation is now forming, I pray and believe, that will walk in an anointing that has never been known by humankind before, including the disciples. This generation won't need natural illustrations to help them understand what their spiritual task is. They will move into spiritual territory that defies the natural order. I said earlier in the book that God wants to give us revelations and experiences of Heaven that have no earthly parallel. Jesus told Nicodemus, *"If I have told you earthly things and you do not believe, how will you believe if I tell you heavenly things?"* (John 3:12).

Jesus had just used two natural illustrations to illustrate the Christian life. One was childbirth, and the other was wind. Then He said He had more to say about spiritual realities that have no earthly parallel. This is important, because we are brokers of a heavenly realm. We are here as ambassadors assigned, given dominion over a planet, to represent His Name, to do what Jesus did. What good are we if we can't understand and operate in the spiritual realm which has no natural parallel? But as the generations embrace their inheritance, I believe we will move into the season Jesus spoke about that defies the natural order. Let me explain.

There are natural principles we live and work by in the things of the Spirit. We understand spiritual things through natural pictures. We compare evangelism to a harvest because we are familiar with the process of plowing a field, making the dirt tender so it can receive seed, then planting, watering, tending, and harvesting. Those are the natural principles of harvest. But Jesus wants us to understand spiritual realities that have no natural picture. Jesus gave such a revelation that defies nature when He said, "... *Behold, I say to you, lift up your eyes and look at the fields, for they are already white for harvest!*" (John 4:35).

He meant that, with a superior revelation not bounded by the natural order, every day is harvest day. There is no waiting for the right season. Those people who seem impossible to win to the Lord will be won instantly, without any sowing or preparation or tending, if our anointing is equal to the revelation Jesus has for us in John 4:35. The anointing on a coming generation will be great enough that the natural order of things will no longer apply. With a low-grade anointing and revelation, we have to live by natural principles and restrictions to get spiritual results. But Jesus brings this revelation which is almost frightening. He says, *"Lift up your eyes,"* meaning, "With the way you see things right now, you cannot operate on the revelation I want to give you. But there is something available for a coming generation where their anointing is so extreme that every person will be ready for harvest."

Jesus walked in such an anointing, carrying the Spirit without measure, that instantly defied the natural principles that illustrated spiritual truths. The more you and I become empowered and directed by the Spirit of God, the more our lives should defy the natural principles that release spiritual realities. It's not that the principles of harvest are no longer true. They are as true as they ever were, but they are superseded by a superior truth. What used to take years or months now takes weeks or days to solve.

Think of the Gadarene demoniac in Mark 5. The Church today would treat a man like that much differently than Jesus did. It wasn't long ago that Christians wouldn't even pray for an insane or deranged person. We sent them to asylums and to doctors to have their problem fixed. Now we at least have the courage to pray for them, and we're seeing breakthroughs. Multiple personality disorders and people who have suffered satanic ritual abuse are made right with prayer, and what used to be beyond our realm of faith now can be broken with the anointing we have.

But I still doubt if we would do what Jesus did: He sent the man into ministry right after being saved! We would probably insist that he go through a longer process of healing and deliverance before being entrusted with the position of being the director of evangelism for that region. With the average anointing we carry as a people, we would have to take him through months of counseling sessions and many training classes to make sure he is *debugged*. But as the anointing increases, it increasingly defies natural laws. You will know it is increasing because it will bump up against the very boundaries and limits of faith you used to live within.

Another example is this: Jesus came up to the fig tree which had no fruit on it. It was not the right season for fruit (see Mark 11:12-14). But He cursed it anyway. Why? Because He has the right to expect impossible fruit. He requires from us fruit that is impossible to bear. I said before, it is not normal for a Christian to not have an appetite for the impossible. It's completely abnormal; it's a deformity that comes through disappointment and/or bad teaching.

Remember the promise out of Amos 9:13,

> *"Behold, the days are coming," says the LORD, "When the plowman shall overtake the reaper, and the treader of grapes him who sows seed; the mountains shall drip with sweet wine, and all the hills shall flow with it."*

That illustrates this very principle. We must lift our eyes to see from His perspective. A greater vision/revelation makes a greater anointing available, if we'll *earnestly pursue spiritual gifts* (see 1 Cor. 14:1).

How do we know we've lifted them high enough? Because we can see differently–everyone ready for harvest. How does the plowman overtake the reaper? The growth stages are <u>no longer restricted by natural laws</u> of planting and harvesting, but have become supernatural in nature. The field is growing at the same time it is being harvested and planted. The seasons are overlapping. Why? Because a generation embraced its spiritual inheritance, and in that new territory the anointing is strong enough to defy natural boundaries the Church has lived within for centuries.

We are to expect & rea God's power breaks all scie rules.

FOLLOW THE GENERALS...

We are in the beginning stages of the season called *accelerated growth*. I believe it is possible under the mercy and grace of God to make up for several hundred years of failure in these areas. It is possible, if we are willing to pour ourselves out, to lay the groundwork for another generation to come and use our ceiling as their floor, to build upon it, to bring things of the Church into a place where it must come to.

Proverbs 13:22 says, *"...A good man leaves an inheritance to his children's children...."* Righteousness causes us to realize that our daily decisions affect several generations away. We must learn to sow into the welfare of a generation we may never live to see.

I think of my father, who was a great general in the army of God. What I and my church are experiencing right now is beyond what I used to dream. But much of it, if not all of it, is because my dad paid a price. I watched him when I was a young man. I watched him push ahead as a forerunner, enduring so much criticism and rejection. He honorably displayed what it looked like to value the presence of God above the opinions and support of man. It cost him severely, but he left a rich inheritance for our family, as well as for the church in our region.

In the final five days of his life, 20 or more family members were with my dad, singing praise and ministering to God, because that's what he taught us. He taught us that in all situations you give honor to God. It's our highest honor to bless His great Name and take delight in Him. He showed us how. So we were with him hour after hour, worshiping, giving glory to God, praying, sharing testimonies, telling family stories, finding time to rest in shifts, and then singing once again. We did this 24 hours a day in a constant cycle. And then he died. And we wept. We did all the things grieving families do. We were so sorry for our loss, happy for his reward.

Then I said to all the family members who were there, "Dad carried a mantle that can't be left here. An entire family must embrace it. We have an obligation to build on his ceiling, not to defend and protect what he accomplished, but to take it to its natural conclusion and to walk in realms of dominion that have been made possible because of his sacrifice." Every individual, from the youngest to the oldest, surrounded the bed before we let anyone take him away, and we prayed, "Lord, we receive that mantle of grace that is on this household because of the price this man paid."

I don't care if you're a first-generation believer, or if your family has been in the Church for generations. By revelation you have access to an inheritance that is beyond your wildest imagination, beyond your wildest dream. We owe it to the generations in the past to occupy that territory because they paid a great price to bring it to us. We owe it to our parents, our grandparents, and to our great-grandparents. We owe it to our children and their children. Before Jesus returns there will be the community of the redeemed walking under the influence of their inheritance, *a city whose builder and maker is God* (see Heb. 11:10).

There will be a generation that steps into the cumulative revelation of the whole Gospel. There will be a generation that lifts their eyes and sees that supernatural season in which every single person is harvestable now, and that has the anointing necessary to carry it out. My cry is to see these things in my lifetime, so I'm giving my life for it. But I have told my kids and the young people I pastor, "If we don't get there together, take it on. Do not be shaped by the opinions of man, but be shaped by your value for His presence. Any price you pay in claiming more territory for God is well worth the exchange."

CHAPTER 7

GRAFTED INTO
THE FAMILY

In this chapter, I want to visit two topics: family inheritance and spiritual inheritance. It's important to understand these two topics as they are relevant and vital to where we are going. In the Old Testament there is a lot of emphasis on inheritance coming from the bloodline of a family. Then when we read through the New Testament, there is a shift: We are grafted into the family of God when we believe in Him, no matter what our bloodline is.

> *Blessed be the God and Father of our Lord Jesus Christ, who **has blessed us with every spiritual blessing** in the heavenly places in Christ, just as He chose us in Him before the foundation of the world, that we should be holy and without blame before Him in love, having predestined us **to adoption as sons by Jesus Christ** to Himself, according to the good pleasure of His will, to the praise of the glory of His grace, by which He made us accepted in the Beloved. In Him we have redemption*

*through His blood, the forgiveness of sins, **according to the riches of His grace**, which He made to abound toward us in all wisdom and prudence* (Ephesians 1:3-8).

Paul explains it simply: We are adopted as sons and daughters and have been blessed with every spiritual blessing according to the riches of His grace. So even if we don't have great bloodlines that are rich with inheritance, we get grafted into the greatest inheritance in the universe.

Often when I teach on this topic of inheritance and momentum, someone will approach me and say, "I don't have an inheritance, and my family is not one to be proud of." My usual response is, "That's perfect!" Of course, they are usually taken aback. The reason it's perfect is because those without a natural inheritance are being completely set up to change history. They have been presented with one of the greatest opportunities of life—to start their own heritage. Quite frankly, it's an opportunity that I will never have.

We serve a redeeming God; He is the God of the redeemed. This very idea of God being a redeemer is one of the most important things for us to understand in our time. Our ability to start a heritage and a legacy is all rooted in the fact that our Daddy loves redemption. Jeremiah 12:15 reads,

And it will come about that after I have uprooted them, I will again have compassion on them; and I will bring them back, each one to his inheritance and each one to his land (NASB).

What a great verse. God will uproot and place us back into our inheritance and land. Some of us are in a position where we don't have much of an inheritance. Well, today is a good day for us. We serve a redeeming God who is in the business of placing us back into our inheritance. The first step is for us to recognize that we have been grafted into God's family, and this is where it all changes for us.

This past year I had the opportunity of interviewing my dad's mom in front of our first- and second-year class in Bethel School of Supernatural Ministry. The purpose of this time was for her to share some of the history and heritage that have helped create the environment that the students are now living in. During this time, she handed out to every student a piece of paper that had a list of family Scriptures. These passages of Scripture were Bible promises that we have embraced and declared over our families through the years. When my grandma handed this paper out, she said, "These are now your promises for you and your families." What took place was she gave the class an inheritance that became theirs. Her ceiling became their floor. It was fun to see the reaction from the class when they realized what they had just received.

Below are some of the verses that are promises that my family members for generations have held onto and released over our homes and lives. Take these verses and declare them over yourself and your families. Let this become your foundation you build on.

..But as for me and my house, we will serve the LORD (Joshua 24:15).

But the plans of the LORD stand firm forever, the purposes of His heart through all generations (Psalm 33:11 NIV).

Let us, Your servants, see You work again; let our children see Your glory (Psalm 90:16 NLT).

For the LORD is good. His unfailing love continues forever, and His faithfulness continues to each generation (Psalm 100:5 NLT).

Children are a gift from the LORD; they are a reward from Him (Psalm 127:3 NLT).

Those who fear the LORD are secure; He will be a refuge for their children (Proverbs 14:26 NLT).

He shows mercy from generation to generation to all who fear Him (Luke 1:50 NLT).

"In the last days," God says, "I will pour out My Spirit upon all people. Your sons and daughters will prophesy, your young men will see visions, and your old men will dream dreams" (Acts 2:17 NLT).

...Believe in the Lord Jesus and you will be saved, along with everyone in your household (Acts 16:31 NLT).

Just recently a woman in our church, who was a student at the time that my grandma shared those Scriptures, came up to me and shared a testimony with me. She had been declaring these verses over her family, and one of her daughters had become a Christian since she embraced those verses as her own. It was so encouraging to hear how someone is starting a heritage by realizing she has been grafted into the family of God! Now she is able to walk in all the things that He has in store for her.

In Hebrews 12:1, we read,

> *Therefore, since we have so great a cloud of witnesses surrounding us, let us also lay aside every encumbrance and the sin which so easily entangles us, and let us run with endurance the race that is set before us* (NASB).

These witnesses are individuals who have laid down their lives for the purpose of the Kingdom; now they are in place to watch the generations after them advance the Kingdom even more. Can you imagine what it would be like to be in Heaven among this cloud of witnesses? I imagine it to be a great celebration of the great men and women of the faith. They get to watch generations after generations build on the things they paid a price for. Oh, how much fun that would be!

I tell people about my own personal heritage. On my dad's side of the family, I am sixth generation in vocational ministry, and on my mom's side, I am fourth-generation Christian. Can you imagine the honor and blessing my ancestors receive as we continue to run the race of faith?! Because of the decisions they made many generations ago, they continue to reap the benefits of their decisions.

One of our greatest investments in life is to make decisions with the generations in mind. The ability to see the bigger picture is necessary to lay a foundation of inheritance for generations we will never see. This is often the very challenge that people struggle to work through—to live a life with this in mind.

The task to intentionally live for generations we will never see is an incredible opportunity and a huge responsibility. I have seen around the world that when people begin to walk in a fresh understanding of an abundant God, they begin to naturally live for generations they will never see. When people are consumed with lack, they often lose the very ability to do this. We often reduce the Christian life to just our own lives. When we begin to teach that the Christian life is just about us, we need to revisit our very understanding of the Kingdom.

When we practically live our lives for future generations, it can easily be seen in the daily decisions we make. History teaches us something: What cost one generation dearly will often cost the next generation nothing. As we begin a heritage, we have to be willing to accept the fact that we may spend our entire lives building something, and then it's the next generation's decision to advance with what we laid down for them.

Since the mid-1990s, we have been experiencing a unique move of God here in Redding, California, at Bethel Church. Countless lives have been touched by this, and we also have seen a real breakthrough in healing and miracles. We now have pages and pages of miracle testimonies of people who have been touched by God and have been healed from anything from a hurt pinky finger to terminal diseases. It has been quite a journey—and a fun one.

What many people don't know about are the decisions that were made 50 years prior to what we are experiencing now. My mom's parents, Gene and Nell, have been a part of Bethel for over 50 years. We often hear them say, "We prayed for over 50 years to see what we now see every day here at Bethel." It's amazing to me to hear that, as well as all the stories of the really tough seasons Bethel weathered. They had many opportunities to leave this church, but through it all, they decided to believe in the prophetic words and the promises of God that the nations would be coming and revival would come. So they positioned themselves in such a way that would eventually help to create an environment where the nations of the world would come to encounter God.

My dad's parents, Earl and Darliene, were the senior pastors of Bethel Church in the 1970s and 1980s. One of my grandparents' life messages was that our number one ministry in life is worship unto God. They carried a love for worship and people that was contagious. The Jesus Movement brought a lot of people to the churches across the world, and many were not ready for them, especially because they didn't dress and act properly, according to the church-goers of that day. There was a bit of tension between the people who attended church and the people who came to church because of the Jesus Movement. My grandparents on both sides of my family took a stand and welcomed them in spite of the ridicule they received.

Recently, I asked my Grandma Darliene, my dad's mom, whether she was surprised at what is happening here in Redding. She said, "No, I knew it was going to happen. Not a lot of people believed me, but I knew." This is a beautiful example of carrying an absolute resolve to stay true to the course, which eventually became a foundation for generations of people to experience an outpouring of the Spirit. When we are able to see what is destined to happen, it empowers us to easily pay the price for it now. The moment we realize that the Christian life is not just about us and our time, but about going from glory to glory, then we readily pay the price now for what's to come.

Jesus was able to endure the cross because of the joy set before Him.

Fixing our eyes on Jesus, the author and perfecter of faith, who for the joy set before Him endured the cross,

*despising the shame, and has sat down at the right hand
of the throne of God* (Hebrews 12:2 NASB).

He saw the ages of time after Him that would be impacted by
the decision He made to die on the cross and be resurrected. When
He saw that, it enabled Him to "pay the price." It is really hard to
pay a price when we don't see the value in doing so. The price that
is paid shows how clearly we see the value of something.

Decisions like this will be carried to the future generations by
the people who were most impacted by them. Looking at the life
of my grandparents and learning about the price they paid creates
a way of thinking that eventually translates into the way I live my
life. The things that they worked hard to accomplish are the very
things that are natural for me to do and at little-to-no cost.

STARTING OUR OWN HERITAGE

Now let's take a look at what we can do in beginning to live a
life that starts an inheritance. I recently interviewed a great friend
of ours, Danny Silk. Currently Danny and his wife Sheri are the
Family Life Pastors at Bethel Church. Danny has written several
books and is a sought-after speaker in the Church and in pro-
fessional settings as well. He carries a revelation and insight into
family, relationships, and people that never cease to amaze us all.
What many people don't realize is the story behind the man.

As Danny was attending school to get his master's degree, one
of his assignments was to do a project on his own life story. As he
began to remember and recount his upbringing, he realized the
craziness and harsh reality that he had to defy to be where he is
today. This process of overcoming is what I want to look at, and I

will pull out some things that I believe will help many others begin to realize what is possible. No matter what, it is possible to create a positive momentum that goes beyond our lives.

When Danny was 7 years old, his parents divorced. His dad was about 25, and his mom was 23. His dad was a young marine with an alcohol problem, which brought much instability to the home. Shortly after the divorce, his mom, Danny, and his younger brother moved to Weaverville, California. They moved there to live with his mom's stepmom and, they hoped, find a man who could be his dad and a husband to his mom.

At the age of 9, Danny found himself being his mom's counselor, trying to comfort her through all the numerous broken relationships she had. Danny's ideas of family were not based out of healthy relationships, but were clearly being shaped by how well a person could perform sexually. This idea was reinforced by his entire family system. When he turned 15, he was given a box of condoms for his birthday by his grandmother.

By the time he had to complete the autobiography for his college course, he could remember at least 20 different men who came through his house as prospective dads. When he was 12, his mom remarried. This marriage lasted about three years. This man had an alcohol problem and was violent. Although neither he nor his brother was ever assaulted, the violence had its effects. Danny's brother became an angry man as well, filled with rage and alcohol, ready to fight anyone who crossed him.

His real dad remains an absolute stranger to both sons. As you might imagine, this created a significant father wound in his life. In Danny's words, "Not worth the trouble, and not worth knowing." In his quest for validation, love, and purpose, he followed the examples laid out for him by his family: sex, partying, multiple relationships, and a sad realization that life was going to continue much as it had been up to now.

At the age of 21, he stepped foot inside a little church called Calvary Chapel on Main Street in Weaverville, California. The church would later change its name to Mountain Chapel. It was there that he gave his life to Christ. What a great day for him, yet the hunger continued for a real family life at its fullest. It was there he got a firsthand experience of what true family looked like. As he looked around this little church in the mountains, he saw whole families. For the first time in his life, he saw husbands caring for their wives and people who had been married to the same person for a long time. That was both shocking and inspiring for him to see.

Danny married Sheri when he was 23. He soon found out that bringing together the collective dysfunction of two lives made for a very challenging marriage. They now share very openly about the trials and real challenges they had as a married couple. However, something in them told them it was possible to have a healthy marriage and family. They had been exposed to it in that little church. During the many years of their own struggling marriage, they held onto this one thing: that it was possible to be married and stay married to "one person."

In my interview with him, he said there were hundreds of times he thought their marriage was over, but he kept going back to this truth: "It's possible to be married to one person." He refused to let go of this possible reality. I asked him what some of the main things were that enabled him to start a heritage and be able to give an inheritance to his children. Here was his answer: "I was driven by a dream that it was possible." There were some major turning points in his life when he gave his life to Christ and when he was exposed to healthy marriages and families, but it came down to this one thing: He had a hope that he could experience it.

As we concluded our interview, he mentioned that, along with the hope of it being possible, he spent a lot of time getting equipped with skill sets that would enable him to walk out the changes he and Sheri would have to introduce into their relationship. What that did was bring his dream from the hope realm into the experience realm. If you need the skill sets to bring what you hope for into the experience realm, I recommend that you get some of Danny's books.[1] In these books you will find keys that will help you begin to lay a foundation in your life and family that will go beyond your time.

HOPE

As I look back on this interview, there are several things that I want to highlight. The first one is obvious—*hope*. Hope is dreaming while awake. This is an extremely powerful force. We can look in history and see different individuals who created a movement or had a big mark on humanity; all of them had a hope for something greater.

In the face of adversity, trial, and pain, they held on tightly to the hope that it was possible. Inheritance is not for the faint of heart. It is for those who are determined beyond normalcy. Something deep cries out for a greater reality. It is here that hope becomes our best friend. In Romans 4:18 we read of Abraham, "*Who, contrary to hope, in hope believed, so that he became the father of many nations, according to what was spoken, 'So shall your descendants be.'*"

Hope is what carried Abraham for all those years as he was waiting for his promise of a son to be fulfilled. We must learn to hope in the midst of our situations, no matter how discouraging or impossible they look. Hope is the mechanism that attracts solutions and ideas for creating momentum. For some, our first battle will be learning to fight for hope. Once we have hope, then the impossible becomes possible. There is a difference between hope and _living hope_. We can always tell if we have living hope in our hearts. That is when we are thriving no matter the circumstance or situation. There is a victory in our hearts even though the battle rages on.

Once hope is ruling our hearts, then comes a focus, which is necessary for creating momentum and inheritance. Hope is what creates the momentum, and focus is what sustains it. When we move to a place of focus, then we begin to attract the things necessary to be successful at whatever we are trying to do. In this context, we begin to do things that will equip us with the practical and spiritual skills needed to alter our own history and our families' histories. This will bring us to the place we dream of—being able to hand to the next generation an inheritance and momentum that will carry them into the future.

ENDNOTE

1. Danny Silk's resources are available at http://lovingonpurpose.com.

CHAPTER 8

LIVING IN
EXTREME SECURITY

*Confidence is motivated by what it can give. Arrogance
is driven by what it can gain.*

Now that we understand that it is God's nature to release favor, abundance, and blessing to His people, let's take a look at what happens when we embrace this truth. It's important to realize that when God does something, it is designed to bring us to a place of extreme security, and in that place of extreme security, we will be able to see the Lord's hand on our lives. If we don't allow God's favor to bring us to that place, then we are liable to use blessing for our own gain.

In 1998, we had Dr. Rodney Howard-Browne speak at our church. He is one of the great revivalists of our day. Dr. Howard-Browne was at Bethel doing five days of consecutive meetings, which are quite an experience and a good one, for sure.

In a typical meeting, he would spend anywhere from one to two hours on just the offering. This was not including worship or the main message. It was actually quite humorous to watch people get so offended at him for spending so much time on the subject of money. I figured if it was an area of offense, then we needed to hear it all the more.

At the time, my wife and I were financially tight, but we felt we were to give $50. It was in my heart to put money in the offering each night. So we wrote a $10 check each night for 5 nights to add up to $50. Throughout the week, I kept hearing the number "500." I thought, "I like that number; that is a good number." On the very last night, a spirit of generosity came into the meeting, and people began to take their jackets, shoes, watches, jewelry, and all kinds of stuff and bring it to the platform. The most valuable possession I had at the time was my new in-dash CD player in my truck. So I ran out into the parking lot, tore out my CD player, brought it up to the front, and placed it on the stage. It was one of those nights that I can remember as a church we made a commitment to live a life of sacrificial generosity.

Some time later, we had friends over for dinner. We had a great time with them eating and fellowshipping. They left our house late that night, and as we were getting ready for bed, we heard a knock on the door. I was in the bedroom. Candace went to the front door; it was our friends who had just left. A few minutes later, Candace came back to the bedroom with a check in her hand. Our friends had just given us a $500 check. What an exciting moment for us. I remember standing there looking at the check and saying to myself, "I am now responsible to never doubt His provision again."

I learned something that night that I work hard to apply to every area of my life. There have been times over the years when this stance of being extremely secure has been tested over and over.

One night my wife and I were doing our finances at the kitchen table. After we were done paying all the bills and the checkbook was balanced, we looked at the bottom line, and let's say it wasn't the most encouraging number to look at. As we sat at the kitchen table, my wife said, "Eric, I am so thankful for you." I replied, "I am so thankful for you." We then spent the next few minutes just giving thanks for the various things, such as our dining table we were sitting at, the house we were living in, our two daughters, our dog lying at our feet, and the list went on. In our moment of thanks, the atmosphere in our house shifted from anxiety and discouragement to a place of joy and peace. It was there we chose to be thankful, and that action allowed us to live in a place of extreme security.

God is all about continual life, and I have a mandate when He blesses me or releases favor to me to let that bring me to a place of extreme security in Him. It is in this place of security that I thrive. To live in extreme security is a choice. Continually making a choice to do this creates a momentum that allows us to experience His extreme security in every area in life. If I fail to make this decision, then I've chosen a lifestyle of insecurity. Unfortunately, this is a choice many make.

Insecure people do interesting things. They will do anything that brings them security, and it either tends to be at the expense of someone else or their relationship with God. Insecure people attempt to build themselves up by using other people—either drawing attention from them or pushing them down. Every person in the world has the incredible desire to be safe and secure, and if we are not equipped with the necessary tools, we often find ways to get a false sense of security—and doing that is unhealthy.

Let's take a look at the subject of the fear of man. The fear of man is often understood as literal fear of others: "I'm scared of you." We find ways to not be scared of people or their opinions by compromising or reacting. However, another angle on the fear of man is, "Not only am I scared of you, but I also get my affection and attention from you." We obtain value from what people say or the opinions they have, whether good or bad.

If our security is primarily based on what others say, we will begin to be guided by circumstances and the people around us instead of operating from a place of authority. Any time I am more concerned with what those around me say or think, I will compromise who I am as a son of the King. The moment I begin to place a higher value on what people say and get my affection and attention from those around me rather than God, I have submitted myself to an insecure lifestyle.

The way I approach the affection and attention of people is by looking at it like the bonus check at the end of the year. It's not my main source of income, but it's a bonus, much like the cherry on top of the ice cream sundae. I desire the attention and affection of God to be my main source of identity and encouragement, and then the words of others are the extra blessing.

"For we have become partakers of Christ if we hold the beginning of our confidence steadfast to the end" (Heb. 3:14). This verse is emphasizing that since we are of Christ, there is a confidence we are to walk in to the end. Remember, confidence is motivated by what it can give; arrogance is driven by what it can gain. These two things are often confused with one another. I often joke with people and say, "Don't confuse my confidence with arrogance." As we begin to move into walking in our inheritance for another generation, it is important to gain our confidence from the King Himself. If we do this right, we will have an army of confident people who will know how to rise above the circumstances and situations they face. Our

inheritance is meant to give us a confidence in Him and enable us to face any situation and thrive.

For centuries, the Church has taught people not to be amazing, and we have been told over and over not to stand out. This is so contrary to Scripture and the life that Jesus lived. It's not accurate or scriptural to teach a generation of people not to be amazing. You will find that Jesus celebrated when His disciples did amazing things. We can read in Luke 10:21 that He worshiped the Father as a result of this. *"In that hour Jesus rejoiced in the Spirit and said, 'I thank You, Father, Lord of heaven and earth....'"* This was a direct result of the Kingdom fruit of the 70 who were sent out to preach the Gospel.

There is this common fear that if we become amazing and truly stand out in society, we may become full of pride. If we're fearful of a possible destination, we will remove ourselves from the supernatural grace to do something well and relegate ourselves to an inferior lifestyle.

The goal is not to be famous or well-known, but to walk in confidence and steward what comes with it. This is an aspect of what it means to be Christ-like. It is fun to study the life of Jesus through this lens of how confident yet humble He was. There were things that He did and said that can be only understood if we can see clearly the core values He operated from. An example would be His reaction to the woman who was caught in the very act of adultery (see John 8:3-12). While the religious leaders were going to stone her as a result of their judgment, He responded in the opposite spirit. Jesus had a different set of core values that dictated how He responded to situations like this. This adulterous woman and the religious leaders in this story were exposed to a new covenant in which things were handled differently.

Something that I see over and over in many people is an insecurity about who they are and what they do. A scary combination is when an insecure person is given any form of power, whether it's influence, money, or resources. Abraham Lincoln said, "Nearly all men can stand adversity, but if you want to test a man's character, give him power."[1]

TWO TYPES OF QUESTIONS

Now let's look at another angle on what we can do to steward our confidence. There are two types of questions that can be asked: We can ask questions to justify and strengthen our doubt or ask questions because we truly desire to know the truth. Let's look at the first type of question. In Matthew 12:38-42 is a conversation that Jesus is having with the scribes and Pharisees:

> *Then some of the scribes and Pharisees answered, saying "Teacher, we want to see a sign from You." But He answered and said to them, "An evil and adulterous generation seeks after a sign, and no sign will be given to it except the sign of the prophet Jonah. For as Jonah was three days and three nights in the belly of the great fish, so will the Son of Man be three days and three nights in the heart of the earth. The men of Nineveh will rise up in the judgment with this generation and condemn it, because they repented at the preaching of Jonah: and indeed a greater than Jonah is here. The queen of the South will rise up in the judgment with this generation and condemn it, for she came from the ends of the earth to hear the wisdom of Solomon: and indeed a greater than Solomon is here."*

In this situation, Jesus refused to answer a question from them when they were immovable in their doubt and unbelief. At this point in His ministry, He was known for His incredible teachings and revelations, for His miracles, signs, and wonders. His name had become a household name for many. The religious leaders of the day were asking for another one of those signs that they had previously seen. Jesus responded simply by saying no and then giving some insight that is key in understanding how to let God's breakthrough bring us to a place of extreme security.

Jesus responded by calling them an "evil and adulterous generation." Their hearts were motivated by an evil intent that could only widen, not close, the gap of unbelief. They also were walking in unfaithfulness in their covenant with God, and they were called an *adulterous* generation because of that. Jesus knew that because of their unfaithfulness in the covenant with God, they were not going to be convinced with another sign. Though they, of all people, were carrying all the knowledge and stories of what God has done, it still did not lead them to a place of believing Him.

So instead of showing them another sign, Jesus responded by giving them two examples. The first example was the prophet Jonah, and the second example was the Queen of the South. What I find interesting is that both of the examples that He used were in the history books. In other words, it happened before their lifetime. Jesus was explaining to them that they were responsible to allow what they know in history to bring them to a place of believing Him.

One of the great mistakes we can make as believers is to carry knowledge about what God has done and not let it transform us. If we fail to let it transform us, then we have set the bar low, and we will remain spiritually the same for the length of our lives. The responsibility that we carry for not just what we have seen in our lives, but also what we have heard in others' lives is startling.

Most people can believe it when they see it. It's another thing to believe once you've heard something. In John 20:29, Jesus said, *"Thomas, because you have seen Me, you have believed. Blessed are those who **have not seen and yet have believed**."* This is a high standard that we are called to live. It's one that few have successfully navigated. It's one thing to believe in something that is physically tangible and makes sense to our logic and reason. It's another thing to be able to walk in a high level of confidence and faith in response to what isn't physically tangible or hasn't happened in our lifetime.

Here Jesus was confronting the scribes and Pharisees about their inability to cross over from unbelief to belief. He made it really clear to them that another sign would do nothing but strengthen their doubt and unbelief. The religious leaders of that day carried a very heavy responsibility since they were exposed to so much truth, yet they remained hard and callous to who was standing in front of them—the Messiah.

Now let's look at the other type of questions—those asked earnestly to know the truth. In John 3, we can read about a man named Nicodemus and how he sought Jesus late one night. Nicodemus was deeply troubled by some of the teachings he had heard from Jesus; he really was searching for answers. I believe that Nicodemus approached Jesus from a position of a pure desire to know Him. We can tell this because of the way Jesus responded to him. Through the course of this conversation, we can see that Nicodemus walked away with what he came for: answers to his questions.

There is nothing wrong with asking questions as long as the motivation is to know the truth. It is important to realize that our ability to continue growing in our understanding of who God is partly lies in our ability to approach Him with this attitude. Many times in life we are confronted with things that challenge our very beliefs and ideas, and it's vital to learn to approach God with the same attitude that Nicodemus carried—and that was to know the truth. So the challenge for us is to learn to carry an attitude that desires to know the truth.

When we are confronted with truth or something that God has done, we are then responsible to _live and act_ according to what we've been exposed to. This is what it means to walk in extreme security. When we live our lives with that truth in mind, even when we are in certain situations, we are only influenced by the truth and not the situation and circumstances. Unfortunately, we often carry the truth into situations, but come out not holding to that truth anymore. This is where we are to be champions of truth and learn to carry it firmly, regardless of what is happening around us. This is a direct result of being extremely secure in what God has done.

As we allow all these things to bring us into a place of extreme security, something unique begins to take place. We begin to see something that we've never seen before. We begin to recognize where and who the hand of Lord is upon. We are no longer driven by our insecurity, and now our security allows us to see clearly where the Lord is and what He is doing.

In 1995, I was in my first year of college and decided to go home for a visit to my family. I walked into the church on a Sunday morning, and my brother was leading worship. As I was sitting there, a jealousy rose up in me because he was up there and I wasn't. It's embarrassing to even think about it now, but I was acting very insecure. It was a long worship service for me as I was really struggling with jealousy.

At one point in the worship service, one of the elders of the church and a good friend came up to me and whispered a word in my ear, "Eric, the Lord has created you to be who you are." I was sitting there thinking, "How does he know this?" I had told nobody of my "issue," but God knew. Instantly I repented of my attitude and realized that I had created a place where a divisive spirit could have a place in my life. My jealousy was bringing division to what God was doing. This issue actually made it impossible for me to recognize the hand of the Lord on my brother's life.

When we allow attitudes like this to take root in our lives, they will blind us and will deprive us from seeing what God is doing. When we are able to be secure and confident in what God says about us, our eyes and ears become really good at recognizing the favor and anointing on someone else's life. This one revelation will forever alter the course of our lives, as it will move us to a place of being givers instead of takers. Instead of acting in ways that seek things for our own selfish reasons, we can act in ways that generously give.

When we begin to live in extreme security, a momentum will be created, and we will begin to fully experience what it means to be the Body of Christ. The environment shifts from what we can get to what the Lord is doing. We begin to embrace when the Lord is moving on somebody else, and there isn't any resistance or issue in our heart—and with this, we step right into the momentum at hand. A spirit of generosity is not concerned about what it can get; it's motivated by the opportunity of giving.

In my early years of ministry, I had a season in which I was contending for more anointing and breakthrough in my life and ministry. I was doing all I knew to do—fasting, praying, having hands laid on me, and reading my Bible. It had been a season of just going after some things in my heart. In my own pursuit of this, I saw the very anointing I was hungry for rest on somebody else in our church. Honestly, it threw me off guard. This particular person was someone I had been pastoring and counseling; his life was a mess. He was addicted to drugs, and he was living an immoral lifestyle. I'm not even sure if he wanted the anointing he got. I know I did.

What a great opportunity for me to celebrate somebody when it really offended me. It's not an issue of getting offended; it's what we do with that offense. I chuckle when people say they don't get offended. My response is, "You just haven't had an opportunity yet." It was in this moment of offense that I had a choice to make. I remember it as clearly as yesterday; I was standing there looking at what had just happened, and in that moment, I had to learn to celebrate what had happened with this young man.

Have you ever been in a season where you're contending for something, whether it be an anointing, a healing, or any type of breakthrough? You do all the things you know to do, but then watch someone else walk into the very thing you're after. This is a great opportunity not to allow jealousy and envy to take root in your heart.

> Now the LORD had said to Abram: "Get out of your country, from your family and from your father's house, to a land that I will show you. I will make you a great nation; I will bless you and make your name great; and you shall be a blessing. **I will bless those who bless you,** and I will curse him who curses you; and in you all the families of the earth shall be blessed" (Genesis 12:1-3).

This is where God makes it really clear to Abram, "My hand of blessing is on you, and if anybody blesses you, I will extend My blessing to them as well." God is giving us an opportunity to receive the blessing that is on someone else's life when we simply bless and honor the one that has it.

It is an incredible privilege to rejoice when someone else gets the breakthrough. My dad always says, "The ability to rejoice in someone else's miracle is the very thing that qualifies you for your own." This is something that we must cultivate in our everyday lives. For some, it may be sacrificial at first, but it will eventually become pure joy to them when someone else receives his or her breakthrough. When we make the decision to rejoice in others' victories and blessings, we and those around us will experience exponential growth.

ENDNOTE

1.   See http://www.quotationspage.com/quote/414.html.

CHAPTER 9

INHERITANCE PROMOTES US TO RESPONSIBILITY

Jesus increased in wisdom and stature, and in favor with God and men (Luke 2:52).

Now that we are moving into a place of recognizing our inheritance, let's look at what is required from us. When we receive an inheritance, it is a promotion to responsibility. We often reduce inheritance to retirement. There tends to be a misunderstanding that when we receive an inheritance it is now time to retire and live off of what we have just received. Often we see in history that one generation has paid a massive price to see something established or take place, but when they hand it off to the next generation, they either mishandle it or receive it as something that they can live off of rather than stewarding it for increase.

CONFRONTING THE SPIRIT OF ENTITLEMENT

One of the challenges we are facing in this day is equipping a generation to fully understand the heavy responsibility of receiving an inheritance. Something that I run into often in different settings is a mindset of entitlement. One of the adverse effects of equipping a generation of people to be confident, powerful, and free is that it can breed a sense of superiority, which is very destructive. The goal is not to become superior, but to become beneficial.

When we look at the life of Jesus, we see an incredible example of what it means to be a powerful person, walking in confidence and living the life of a servant. In our modern-day culture, we equate confidence and power with a way to climb up the ladder of spirituality to be Number One. Something that I mention often is, *the greater the anointing we carry, the greater the level of service is required.* The point is, as we grow in our identity in Christ, a desire is placed within us to be a blessing to those around us.

PROCESS VS. STRIVING

One of the areas we need to look at is gaining a healthy understanding of process. This can be theologically challenging for many reasons. The argument is that when Jesus died on the cross and rose from the dead, there was a complete shift from an old covenant to a new covenant, so we no longer have to do anything to get what He has made available. With this reasoning, we have removed process from the equation. We then move from a place of responsibility to a place of entitlement. It is in this place that we see many people abusing or misusing their inheritance. This is a hurdle that the generations in the past and the generations to come will need to jump over.

It's necessary for us to understand the difference between process and striving. A lot of the things that Jesus confronted were mindsets and issues of the heart. When this is done correctly, we will see process at its best. If this is done incorrectly, we will see striving at its worst. Process helps prepare us and our hearts to recognize what we have and to use it in a way that honors the King.

What does process look like? In my life I have seen it in two ways. One, I go through process before I am ready to receive what the process is for. Conversely, I am given the very thing I'm not ready for, and that is what teaches me to carry it well. The question is not why one happens and the other doesn't, but what I am going to do with what is in front of me.

Let's take a look at the disciples and how much Jesus trusted them to carry power and authority.

> *Then He called His twelve disciples together and gave them power and authority over all demons, and to cure diseases. He sent them to preach the kingdom of God and to heal the sick (Luke 9:1-2).*

Some amazing things take place in this chapter. They feed the 5,000, see a demon-possessed boy get set free, and see Jesus transfigured on the mount. Jesus also catches them talking about who is the greatest among them. One city they go to rejects Jesus. In reaction to that, James and John want to commit mass murder by wiping out the entire city with thunder and lightning. The way Jesus responds to these situations is quite different than the way we would have reacted. Instead of benching them, Jesus continues on in ministry with these guys. In fact, He doesn't slow down at all. In Luke 10:1, we read, *"After this the Lord appointed seventy-two others and sent them two by two ahead of Him to every town and place where He was about to go"* (NIV).

So even after the disciples displayed what we would call character issues, Jesus commissions 70 more of them to go out and preach the Kingdom. Jesus operated differently than we do in many ways. Does it mean that He didn't care about character issues? No, in fact, He spent a good amount of time preaching and teaching on such things. But He was completely fine with giving a group of people the power and authority to do all these supernatural things before we would think they were ready. His process is different than ours. Jesus seems to like the hands-on approach. learning / growing through working, but not book re

The religious spirit is what produces striving, and grace is what produces process. The Pharisees and Sadducees were spending their time striving to have good form, but the disciples were in process of calibrating their hearts. The spirit of religion is purely focused on form and avoids addressing the issues of the heart. In other words, it's form without power. Once our attention is drawn away from calibrating our hearts, we will then need something externally to guide us in our lives.

If process was not necessary for us, then we might as well throw out the teachings of Jesus and the rest of the New Testament. In Paul's books, he spends a great deal of time giving guidance and correction to churches about how to live life, and he addresses the issues of the heart along with behavior. It's not an issue of having to go through process to receive salvation; it is for the purpose of learning how to carry what He gave us. We would not be able to handle all the glory of God if He were to give it to us now. The sheer weight and impact that would have on us would kill us. As we calibrate our hearts, something takes place, and we learn how to carry the presence of God well.

Let's read how Jesus actually went through process as well:

Now His parents went to Jerusalem every year at the Feast of the Passover. And when He became twelve, they

went up there according to the custom of the Feast; and as they were returning, after spending the full number of days, the boy Jesus stayed behind in Jerusalem. But His parents were unaware of it, but supposed Him to be in the caravan, and went a day's journey; and they began looking for Him among their relatives and acquaintances. When they did not find Him, they returned to Jerusalem looking for Him. Then, after three days they found Him in the temple, sitting in the midst of the teachers, both listening to them and asking them questions. And all who heard Him were amazed at His understanding and His answers. When they saw Him, they were astonished; and His mother said to Him, "Son, why have You treated us this way? Behold, Your father and I have been anxiously looking for You." And He said to them, "Why is it that you were looking for Me? Did you not know that I had to be in My Father's house?" But they did not understand the statement which He had made to them. And He went down with them and came to Nazareth, and He continued in subjection to them; and His mother treasured all these things in her heart. And Jesus kept increasing in wisdom and stature, and in favor with God and men (Luke 2:41-52 NASB).

What I find interesting in the last verse is that it says Jesus increased in *"wisdom and stature, and in favor with God and men."* It's important to understand that this was necessary in the unfolding ministry of Jesus. The life that He lived and the things that He did were based on His growth in wisdom, stature, and favor. If

Jesus, being completely human, had to go through process in these three areas, then it shouldn't surprise us if we do as well.

If we know history, we will have a lot of good information, but if we understand history, we will create our own. One of the things that is a lost art in our increasingly rapid world is the ability to build slowly. Our pace of life demands we move quickly and produce on the spot. That is fine, and I actually enjoy a nice full pace, personally. However, when we are creating an inheritance and building a legacy, it often requires a much slower approach. There is a temptation to build *big,* but not build *deep.*

We often remind ourselves that we don't want to become bigger on the outside than we are on the inside. With the advent of media and social networking, there is a major pull to become bigger than we really are. If we can begin to build *slow* and build *deep* in a society where that is often disregarded, then we are about to see an explosion of inheritance and revival go beyond what we thought was possible. If a generation of people can avoid being driven by what is available and instead be driven by building a personal history, then watch out. Something unprecedented is about to happen.

Mike Bickle has noted that this generation alive today will be the most powerful generation because, in the midst of all the options of what they could do, they say yes to the one thing, and it will propel them beyond what any other generation has done.[1]

SELF-PROMOTION

Self-promotion is usually rooted in our lack of trust in God. One of the toughest things to address in our modern culture is this topic of self-promotion. There is such an emphasis in our day and age on being known and finding ways to get known. As we look at the life of Jesus, we see a different approach to life. It's important to understand how Jesus approached life and ministry and to make the necessary adjustments.

It's hard to find a place where Jesus intentionally promoted anything He did to attract larger crowds or become a household name. In fact, He made statements or did things that actually discouraged crowds from following Him. For example, He made statements like this:

> Whoever **eats My flesh and drinks My blood** has eternal life, and I will raise him up at the last day. For My flesh is food indeed, and My blood is drink indeed. He who eats My flesh and drinks My blood abides in Me, and I in him (John 6:54-56).

Notice how He didn't really bother to explain what He meant by *"eat My flesh and drink My blood"* to the multitudes before they left. It's easy for us to embrace it because later Jesus explains what this means to His 12 disciples—communion. The crowd's reaction to that statement was that they left that gathering entirely. If He wanted to be well received, then this certainly was not something to say in public.

It's very clear that growing a large ministry and becoming a well-known person was not His motivation. Something else motivated Him; it was doing exactly what the Father was doing. When people are like Jesus—very secure in who they are and fully aware of how Daddy sees them—they will have absolutely no need to promote themselves. They will carry a presence and favor about them that will open the doors and create the momentum for them. Instead of trying to open doors, the doors will be opened.

This momentum that we are referring to is being created in the Body of Christ, and it will ride on the shoulders of ones who have no need to promote themselves. Any time people begin to move into self-promotion, it can usually be traced back to the simple reality that they don't trust God. This causes them to come to a place where they feel the need to do something about it, and they then move into promoting themselves. We have to learn to let the favor of God and the favor of people open the doors. As we learn to let our hearts be calibrated to the heart of God, we will then lead an entirely different life. We will be motivated by what we can give, and we will lead with our hearts. As Larry Randolph says, "Don't let your gift lead your heart, but let your heart lead your gift."[2]

EXTENDING OUR BLESSING

Recently my wife and I were doing a conference in another country, and during the day we were meeting with the leaders with regard to the church they were getting ready to launch. The unique thing about this particular situation was that the majority of the leaders who were planting the church were a family: Dad and Mom and their three kids. They are all very actively involved in the creation and launching of this church within this community of people they had been meeting with for a few years.

At one point in the conversation, we chatted about the interesting dynamic of other leaders finding their place in that environment where a majority of the leadership is a family. As we began to talk about some of the issues and things that they were working on, a comment came up from one of the adult children: "I can feel that the other people think I am in leadership because I'm a daughter of the senior leaders." Because of this she was wondering if she should step down or step to the side to allow the others to rise up as leaders.

In this specific situation, the daughter who made the comment carried an anointing, and from our perspective she was to be on the leadership team even though she was part of the family. I then told her it was important that she not turn away something that is her inheritance.

She then asked, "Well, what should I do about this as it is hard to figure it out?"

My reply was, "It's important to find ways to extend your blessing and inheritance to others around you."

When we truly walk in our inheritance, we also walk in authority in a natural realm and a spiritual realm. One of the responsibilities of having favor, inheritance, and blessing is mastering how to extend it to those around us. It's learning how to be extremely generous with what we have been given. Some practical things we will look at are prayer, opportunities, and relationship.

PRAYER OF BLESSING

When we have authority, we don't find ourselves asking for permission to do something; we walk in complete confidence to do what we carry. One of the key things in relation to a prayer of blessing is the position of authority we pray from, and that is from the *heavenly places* (see Eph. 2:6). When we are seated in heavenly places, we are living from a place of no lack and extreme abundance. Our awareness of how blessed we are leads us to a place where we can give it away. We can only give what we have. When people carry a certain measure of the blessing of the Lord, they are in a position of authority to give it away. So let's take this same principle of authority and apply it to this realm of inheritance.

There is a man named Hakon Fagervik in Norway whom I met last year. Hakon is a very humble and gracious man. His heart burns for Scandinavia, and he is a spiritual father in the region. Some time ago, he was asked by a friend of his to come and pray a prayer of blessing for his new fishing boat. At the time the fishing industry in this town in the northern part of Norway was suffering, and the economy was taking a hit because of this. So Hakon made the trip up to this fishing village. He said he anointed the boat with oil and prayed a simple prayer of blessing and blessed his friend's fishing boat. What happened next is history.

The friend ended up bringing in loads of fish while the other boats didn't do very well. The word got out that Hakon had prayed over this man's boat and that this was the reason for its success. Some time later, Hakon was visiting the area, and some of the other fishermen heard that he was around, so they asked him if he could pray over their boats. Sure enough, he prayed over the boats, and guess what happened? Yep, they too began bringing in large catches. Then the word really got out, and pretty soon all the businesses and hotels asked him to pray a prayer of blessing over their community. The impact of this was so great that the local newspaper ran a story on the whole thing and explained how the economy of the region turned around simply because of Hakon's prayer.

What a great testimony of how to extend inheritance to those around us! One of the great things we can do to extend what we carry is to simply release it in prayer over others. This is often done, but not often realized. When we begin to realize and carry an understanding of the power of prayer in this context, we will be amazed. I have seen many times the circumstances in a person's life completely changed for the good simply because of a prayer of blessing. Thus, one of the first things we, as carriers of this authority, can do to extend blessing to those around us is to release it to them in prayer.

GIVING AWAY OPPORTUNITIES

My dad taught me something years ago. He said, "My kids will pay a price for who I am, so I need to make sure they get opportunities because of who I am." Our blessing and inheritance has the ability to become a bridge to allow others to cross over and experience firsthand what we live in. One of the ways to do this is allow others to experience the opportunities that we get to experience. We must create ways to share experiences that are directly related to who we are.

One of the things I consider a complete honor and blessing is to hang out with various "revival generals" who are alive today. They often come to Bethel to speak in our school or at a conference. When it is appropriate, I will invite one of my staff members or a student to come along for a lunch with one of these generals. It's fun to see their reaction to sitting across the table from a general, and how they absorb the moment as much as they can. Something that I get access to all the time is also something that I can use as a bridge for the people in my life to experience as well.

RELATIONSHIP THAT COVERS

What I feel the Lord is doing in the earth is helping us to better understand what it means to cover each other in relationship and community. I believe that this is the most powerful way to extend blessing to someone else. When we come into a relationship with God through Jesus, we are then entrusted with the Kingdom. This is the *great exchange.* That's pretty stunning. In this very act of giving our lives, we are positioned for Him to give us the Kingdom from an eternal realm. When we come into a relationship with God, He gives us access to *all spiritual blessing* (see Eph. 1:3). What a deal!

This is the ultimate inheritance. What's so amazing about this is that no matter what background or upbringing we have, we get the same thing as those who have a deep Christian heritage. Wow! I have heard and read stories of people and what they have done in the Kingdom, and often they are people who have all the reasons necessary to do nothing because of their dysfunctional background or the horrible upbringing they had. Instead they tapped into a realm of inheritance and lived from there. They refused to let their past determine their future.

Recently, we attended a family reunion in Park City, Utah. What a great time we had reconnecting and meeting parts of the family that we hadn't seen or met in 22 years since our last reunion. One of the things we did was hire a couple of guys to come and film different members of the family to capture our present-day lives and stories so we could keep records of them for now and the future generations. My dad and I were asked to do an interview together.

One of the questions I was asked was, "Can you explain how the deep and rich spiritual inheritance has been passed down so successfully in your family now for six generations?"

My reply was, "There's no pressure to be something you're not, and there is a tremendous amount of freedom to be who you are."

As I look back on my life, I can't remember when my parents told me what to do with my life. There wasn't any time spent in discussing what they expected from me as far as a career, where I would go to school, or what kind of job I should get. They poured their lives into the attitudes of my heart and my character as a person.

Often when an inheritance is passed on, some expectations are passed along with the inheritance as well. Even though this may be done with good intentions, it sometimes can be unhealthy. So for the generations of my family, this value for focusing on connection and relationships has created a great amount of freedom for individuals to carry this inheritance without the pressure of expectation. When we live in the fullness of relationship, there is no need for external pressure to get us to do something. Control is no longer necessary, and the attitudes of our hearts will help us carry inheritance well.

ENDNOTES

1. Mike Bickle, email to Eric Johnson on January 2, 2011.

2. Larry Randolph, email to Eric Johnson on March 17, 2011.

CHAPTER 10

DEVELOPING POWERFUL PEOPLE

We stand on the shoulders of those who have gone before us. —Anonymous

Our current understanding of inheritance in our era looks something like this: We receive our inheritance when a certain person passes away. However, let's take a look at how inheritance was handled in ancient Jewish times. The protocol for inheritance was that when the father felt that his heir had come of age and was ready, he would give the heir the authority to help manage their wealth while he was still alive. This created a generational overlap that made it possible for the heir to learn from his father how to manage it as well as step into a momentum stretching from one generation to the next.

A common expression that we use here at Bethel is, "We stand on the shoulders of those who have gone before us." This chapter is going to touch on some things that will help the next generation begin to do this. One of the signs, in the years to come, that we have been successful in our pursuit of revival will be a generation that is able to take what was given to them and see it increase. We will focus on this process by showing how to "grow" powerful people.

Our goal is not to have a generation stand on the corpses of those who have gone before us. We must stand on the *shoulders* of those who have gone before us. It's a challenge to find past revivals and movements that had a strong emphasis on sons and daughters being raised up in such a way to help lead the revival or movement to the next generation. Let's be diligent in our time to change that.

In this chapter, I will be using the phrase *powerful people*. By this, I mean people who are fully empowered to be who they are and are free of constraints that limit them, but at the same time are serving the environment and people around them.

EMPOWERING STRUCTURES

Then He spoke a parable to them: "No one puts a piece from a new garment on an old one; otherwise the new makes a tear, and also the piece that was taken out of the new does not match the old. And no one puts new wine into old wineskins; or else the new wine will burst the wineskins and be spilled, and the wineskins will be ruined. But new wine must be put into new wineskins, and both are preserved. And no one, having drunk old wine, immediately desires new; for he says, 'The old is better'" (Luke 5:36-39).

This is the parable of the wineskin and the wine. There are numerous things Jesus is teaching in this simple parable. He explains that if we have new wine, we need to make a new wineskin to hold it. Then He goes on to explain that we can't take new wine and put it into an old wineskin or else the new wine will cause the old wineskin to break: It would be no longer usable, and the wine would be wasted. However, when the new wineskin and the new wine come into contact with each other, something powerful takes place. As the wine and the wineskin make contact with each other, a reaction takes place that allows the wine to be stored and protected, and what was a leather pouch has now turned into a wineskin.

Another thing that He is addressing is that new wine determines the need for a new wineskin. In order to better steward the new wine, we need to build a wineskin or structure that is capable of holding that new wine. New wine cannot be expected to be stewarded in an old wineskin or structure. They will likely destroy each other.

When a new wineskin was made, it also created a way for the wine to be drunk now and also be saved for another time. As we begin to build a new wineskin, it's important to do it with an understanding that we are meeting a short-term goal, which is for the present, as well as a long-term goal, which is for the future. Also, what we set up now is going to bring refreshing and life later on.

The wineskin can also be understood as the *structure* that houses the new wine. One of the main reasons that the Kingdom increased on the earth after Jesus ascended back to His Father was that He developed a structure with His disciples, who in turn stewarded the wine and saw it increase in their time.

CULTURE OF RELATIONSHIPS

One of the beautiful things we are experiencing in this movement is the deep level of relationships and commitments that our generals and leaders are making with each other. They have an incredible value for creating and establishing relationship. They are making commitments to serve each other and are coming together solely for that purpose. In looking at revival history, we can see that when we remove the value for relationship, we begin to build our own kingdoms. Randall Worley has said, "All revelation grows in the soil of relationship; otherwise, it is synthetic and not systemic."[1]

The Kingdom is designed on the concept of family. Jesus referred to God as His Father, and He knew that He was the Son. The success of Jesus' ministry came from this place of being a Son in right relationship with the Father. And because of this, the Kingdom would come to earth and advance. This is something that is often overlooked when we read the life of Jesus. It is vital to understand that Jesus walked in relationship with His Father and lived it out in His life with the disciples.

When we live from a core value of relationship, we learn how to take the calling and duty on our lives and work it out with those with whom we are in relationship. We need to stop sabotaging relationship for the sake of the calling on our lives. If we don't confront this problem, we will continue to sweep something under the rug that will need to be addressed later. In order to be truly covered and sent, we must learn to work out our passion, calling, and revelation within the relationships we have. As we move away from sabotaging relationships, we will tap into a reservoir of the Kingdom that will provide the Church with a newfound understanding of inheritance and life that will continue through time.

Currently my role at Bethel is being the Senior Overseer for the second-year program at our Bethel School of Supernatural Ministry (BSSM); I also oversee Bethel International, which is our missions department. These two departments put me in a position where I am exposed to people who are passionate and hungry for revival to spread all over the world. As we process and facilitate deploying revivalists out into the world, something common happens: People are looking for validation to be covered and sent out by Bethel.

This is a great opportunity to look at a culture of relationships and see how it plays into this. The most common reason people ask to be covered and sent out is that no one wants to go out by themselves or do it alone. They desire to be sent. It's in relationship that we are covered and get validated. Walking in relationship with someone or some group of people is what creates a level of intimacy and connection where there is no question whether we are covered or will be sent out to Starbucks or to the continent of Africa. There is no record of the disciples asking Jesus, "Can You send us or cover us?" We can see in Mark 16:15 that Jesus instructs them to *"Go into all the world and preach the gospel...."* This is a very popular verse in the Church as we use it for motivation to travel the planet to preach the Gospel.

Here we have a group of men who have spent three years with Jesus. These three years were unique years in their lives. It was the ultimate team-building experience anybody could have. What they saw and experienced in those three years was astounding and worthy of enough books to cover the earth.

The things they got to participate in and learn about as they lived life with Jesus were unprecedented. At the end of those three years, they knew amazing and quirky things about each other. They knew that Peter was always going to be the first one to open his mouth. They knew that John thought he was Jesus' favorite. They knew all about the sons of thunder. These men grew to know each other very well. So when Jesus instructed them to "Go," it was done out of being in relationship with Him, which gave them validation and covering. Jesus wasn't sending acquaintances out into the world. He was sending His own men out to preach the Gospel, and the impact of their having been sent out through relationship is still affecting the world today.

As we begin to receive our inheritance and release it to the next generation, it is important that we learn how to carry a revelation from the Lord and honor the relationships we have. God is so moved by our ability to honor the relationship we have with Him as well as with the people around us. When we begin to place a higher value on relationship than our duty, we will remove any potential to treat people in an inferior manner. It will affect the way we share the good news with people. Instead of treating them like targets for the Gospel, we will treat them the way people should be treated.

FREEDOM VS. CONTROL

As we create a culture of relationship, it's essential to take a look at two different mindsets that affect how people react to an environment where freedom and empowerment are of high value.

Let's first take a look at the freedom mindset. This is what it looks like: The light is green until it turns red. We walk with a sense of freedom and empowerment to make decisions in the framework of relationship. Unless we have a word from the Lord with a very specific direction, we feel free to make a decision.

My wife and I have operated with this understanding. We can look back at any of our major to minor decisions in life, and there were certain ones when we felt strongly that the Lord had spoken to us on what we were to do. Then there were the others when we didn't have a specific word from the Lord, so we felt a liberty to look at all the options and make a decision that we felt was right. It's almost like God says, "I will honor whatever decision you make."

When we have a freedom mindset and we get around other powerful people, we feel even more powerful and free. Look at the disciples in the Gospels. Why did they argue about who was the greatest in the Kingdom? It's because they felt powerful and free around Jesus. It got so empowering that the moms got involved and asked Jesus if their sons could be the ones who sit next to Him when He sits on the throne. Somehow being around Jesus and being in His environment created such an atmosphere of freedom that they felt like they could take on the world. James and John got to the point where they were about to call thunder down on a city that rejected Jesus. What's the point? When we hang around Jesus, it shouldn't surprise us if we feel incredible—like we can do anything.

This is not something we are used to in our lives. I hear often of friends and people, in the workplace, who share how dumb, scared, insecure, and undermined they feel when they are around their boss. Unfortunately, this has become a common standard in our world that when people are in authority, the rest of us don't typically feel free and powerful when we are around them. We

love & intimacy w/ Jesus

157

need to remember that is not how the Kingdom works. When we live in the Kingdom, we will feel very empowered and free.

Now let's talk about the control mindset. Using the stoplight analogy, this mindset operates this way: The light is red until it turns green. People with this mindset think, "I need to be controlled to do something." Usually people who carry this mindset need to control the people around them to do something, so they need to be controlled as well. This is a very disempowering way of life. Unfortunately, many people live in this reality.

One of the reasons people with a control mindset don't feel free to make decisions is that they are afraid of doing something wrong—so they need someone else to validate the decision for them, or they need someone to tell them what to do. If these same people are put around a powerful person who is very empowering, an interesting dynamic takes place. These people tend to get frustrated because they are waiting to be validated or told to do something—when all along the powerful person is more interested in those people discovering the freedom in Christ and cultivating their dreams and passions.

A common theme throughout Scripture is that God is extremely empowering and is all about freedom. It starts in the Garden of Eden and continues through the New Testament. In Genesis, God created a Garden for Adam and Eve, and it had one tree that produced the forbidden fruit. Instead of making the Garden sin-proof, He took the risk of trusting and empowering Adam and Eve to make a decision. Just as it is His nature to allow us to live in freedom, it also means that we as fathers, mothers, and leaders need to live in and to teach those around us to operate from a mindset that produces freedom and empowerment.

RESPONSIBILITY AND OWNERSHIP

As we develop a culture or structure for empowering people and allowing them to be powerful, the next step is to begin to instill in them a core value of responsibility and ownership.

My parents often reminded me when I was growing up that being responsible would give me privileges. When I turned 16 and was getting my driver's license, Dad and Mom sat me down and explained to me that since I showed them that I knew how to be responsible, I would get the privilege of driving their car. So I knew that in order for me to drive their car, I had to make sure that I kept a high standard of responsibility in my life. That was a great way to keep me motivated in being responsible.

Everybody loves privileges, but not all love responsibility. One of the goals as people and leaders is to help instill responsibility. One of the challenges of a "free" environment is that it is human nature to explore the realm of freedom to unhealthy extremes. The apostle Paul addresses this numerous times in his books. In the Book of Galatians, he writes a letter to a church whose members had broken free from the law, rules, and regulations and who were experiencing freedom in Christ. A result of this newfound freedom was that some individuals were taking this freedom too far.

Whenever people who have been in a prison cell for a long time are released, they are most likely going to try to experience their freedom as much as they can. They no longer have a prison cell to tell them what to do. They now have a thing called *love* to tell them what to do. So Paul teaches in Galatians 5:13 not to allow this new freedom in Christ to give them permission to indulge in the desires of their flesh, but to make sure this new freedom they have is aimed at each other. Let love determine our freedom.

Love replaced the Ten Commandments. The Ten Commandments are very specific about what we are not to do and what we are to do. This set of very good rules was in effect for many years until Jesus came and paid the price for our sins. Jesus came and replaced the law with love. The reason for this is that when we truly love, we won't commit adultery, we won't murder, we won't do the things the Ten Commandments instructs us not to do.

So one of the first things to notice in helping to increase responsibility in the life of others is to make sure we are operating out of a heart of love. Any time my love is disconnected from my responsibilities, I know I'm setting myself up for burnout. One of the key ways to help people take responsibility is to teach (1) them to _operate out of_ a heart of love. We must ask this question: *Is my love connected to what I do?* The answer will reveal how we operate and live our lives.

Love encompasses all the tools we need in order to live a joy-filled, highly successful life. This is why it is the supreme commandment in the new covenant. Love is the very thing that wiped out all requirements of the old covenant. Love will tell us when to say yes and when to say no. Love will create such a security in us that we will be unshakeable.

One of the keys to seeing people in any environment carry (2) ownership and responsibility is _trust._ Trust is vital in any environment that expects to raise up a generation of powerful people. Trust comes from a core value that _people are good._ When we begin to view people from this perspective, we lead and interact with them in a way that builds ownership and responsibility in those around us.

Trust begins with us. If we don't create cultures of trust, then we will usually create cultures that attract people who need to be told what to do, and we will find ourselves micromanaging those around us. This can be seen in any realm of society. Most people wonder why they have to micromanage those around them. It often can be traced to the mindset that they don't trust people and that they don't believe that people know how to make good decisions.

The moment I can move in the direction of trusting people, I start believing that people have the ability to contribute to the world around them. I now start releasing freedom and empowerment to those around me. The effects of this decision will be evident in that people will take full responsibility and ownership for what they do.

STAY HIDDEN

One thing I love about the life of Jesus is that He never had the need to promote Himself. It's an intriguing thought. In an age and time when there is an underlying desire and need in our culture to be known, we have created a habit of looking for ways to promote ourselves or make ourselves known. Yet Jesus never once made Himself known. He was trying to get away from the people to be alone. He would tell people, "Please don't tell anybody what happened to you." (See Matthew 9:27-31.)

In Matthew 6, Jesus mentions several times that for what we do in secret, He will reward us openly. He was making reference to the religious practices of that day in which, when people prayed, they made sure they went to the street corners to proclaim their prayers so everybody within earshot could hear them. Also, when they fasted, they carried themselves in such a way that people knew they were fasting. Jesus was addressing an issue of the heart. Our identity will reveal our ability to keep secrets. Self-promotion usually comes from a lack of trust in God.

What is *fear of man*? As we said earlier, for most people, it involves this kind of thinking: "I am scared of people or of what somebody around me thinks or says about me." This is true, but it also means, "I have a higher value for what people say or think about me than for anything else." It is a mindset that puts the opinions and affections of those around us at a higher value than what God says or thinks about us.

Jesus got all His emotional strength, courage, and security from His relationship with His Daddy. When He came into the world, there was no need to make Himself known to gain any security or emotional strength from those around Him. He walked in a complete, full sense of security in who He was based on how God saw Him. What we see in the life of Jesus is a man who walked in a Kingdom confidence that changed the world.

There was a season when the Lord was highlighting this to me, and it was an issue that I had to confront in my own life. In 1999, my wife and I moved back to Weaverville to be associate pastors at the church I had grown up in, which was the same church my parents pastored for over 18 years. As associate pastor, I was also the youth pastor. Just like any normal youth group, ours met every Wednesday for our weekly gathering.

It wasn't long before I realized that the pressure of preaching every week was going to be an issue with me. I quickly recognized that my ability and desire to preach was very minimal. It wasn't that I had a fear of public speaking; it was that I didn't have anything to say. The first few months went fine as I was able to preach, and the youth group continued to grow spiritually and in attendance. But there came a point when I was out of things to say. I had emptied my tank. When I realized this, I quickly made adjustments; I had the worship team go a lot longer on youth nights. We would worship and worship, but all the while it was one of the ways of my avoiding having to preach. Then when it was finally time to end worship, I would go straight into ministry time and not preach. Honestly, we had some great nights when I did this, but not many knew what I was doing.

Then I began to realize something had to change quickly. I began to seek the Lord, and this was my prayer, "God I need help! I need a desire to preach. I don't know how to do this." This of course was done with a fair amount of emotion. After I had quietly sought the Lord for around six months, the breakthrough came. We had a guest speaker by the name of Judah Smith, who is currently the senior leader of City Church in Seattle, Washington. He is one of my favorite preachers; he is very good at what he does and carries a great anointing to preach.

It was a Sunday morning service. After he finished preaching, he was ministering to our congregation. At one point, he called out, "Where's Pastor Eric?" so I went up to receive ministry from him. He gave me a prophetic word: "The Lord is going to change the way you study and preach." I can't tell you how happy I was to hear that. In the next 24 hours, I felt a complete transition from not having any desire to study and preach to a fire that burned within me to study and preach.

As I began to walk in this new passion to study and preach, something else took place. I found myself constantly looking for approval on how the sermon went. I never directly asked somebody for feedback on the message; it would be done subtly in a conversation with my young people or leadership after the service. I would say, "I'm not sure how that went," or "That didn't come out the way I wanted it to." It was my way of getting affection and approval from those around me on how well I did. I began to get my value from those around me and not from God, and it created a hunger for affection and approval. It became my lifeline, and it wasn't long until I realized that I had now created an appetite for this, and it was becoming a problem.

Colin Powell once said, "Avoid having your ego so close to your position that when your position fails, your ego goes with it."[2]

In our environment, we wouldn't use the word *ego* as much as we would use the word *identity*. If our personal identities are wrapped up in what we do in our lives, and if what we do doesn't go well, our identities crumble. The decision to get our affection and approval from those around us is a sure-fire way to invite a collapse. Our identities cannot be in what we do, but rather in who we are. If we can stay in that place of who we are, it will naturally determine what we do.

As God began to confront this issue of the fear of people in my life, I had to step into a journey to break free from it. I had to learn how to come into the secret place of a more intimate relationship with Him. It was there I had to get my emotional strength and my affections. It didn't happen overnight; it was a process that took some time to break free from lies and habits that I had created.

Staying hidden is paramount to our success in being powerful and free. The Lord wants to trust us with more, but we need to be able to be trusted with the secret place. One of the chief responsibilities of any generation that carries an inheritance is to cultivate a desire to stay hidden.

ENDNOTES

1. Randall Worley, email to Eric Johnson on December 14, 2010.

2. Colin Powell, http://www.nytimes.com/1995/09/17/opinion/liberties-colin-powell-rules.html.

CHAPTER 11

THE END GAME

BILL JOHNSON

A promise from God is not a magic coin for us to cash in at will. It is an invitation to a process. And whether that promise is concerning our inheritance or is in simple response to our petitions, God gives it to us because He is good and He loves us. It is His nature to give. When we embrace His promises, we say yes to a process that prepares us for the answer. Some promises reach maturity rather quickly. In those moments, it usually only requires us to say yes to God and express a confidence that what God has said will come to pass. And quickly it does.

But other promises are much bigger—bigger in the sense that they require more from the person on the receiving end. They require that we offer God a bigger *container of character,* one that is refined and developed so that the answer will not be lost through immaturity. For only with character can blessing be managed well. Gifts are free, but maturity is expensive.

Larry Randolph told us a number of years ago, "While God will fulfill all of His promises, He is not obligated to fulfill our potential." Much of what we need in life will be brought to us. But much of what we want we will have to go get. Much has been made available to us through God's covenant. But it is not automatic. Learning to be hungry and dream, followed by confident pursuit, is one of the most important parts of this Christian life.

While all of God's promises are given to bless people and bring glory to God, some will actually do damage to the people they're released to if those people are not properly prepared. If we think people get messed up after abusing natural wealth, multiply the dangers by a thousand to see the potential damage of abusing spiritual wealth. But then, so are the benefits exponentially greater when we correctly steward the spiritual.

We are a people with promise written in our DNA. Hungering for more is natural and is a sign of life. We have to experience a lot of disappointment or sit under bad teaching to be removed from the continual expectation of good happening throughout our walk with Christ. Misunderstanding the process of development causes many to either mistrust God or, at minimum, mistrust their ability to come into all that God has promised.

But learning to pursue more is a huge part of the Christian life. It is the Promised Land of old, the city whose builder and maker is God. It is what the prophets spoke about, what Jesus actualized, what the apostles tasted of and laid down their lives for. It is this glorious journey with Jesus that is filled with ups and downs, successes and failures, and abundance and need.

It is this life for which we were designed. We are a people whose primary focus is the goodness of God. And from that reference point, we have the privilege to live life to the fullest, paying whatever price is necessary to obtain all that God has promised. This joyous journey is the greatest of honors in serving God.

ACCESSING THE KINGDOM

There are two basic approaches for advancement in the Kingdom that pertain to the subject of spiritual inheritance. They are unique and specific, speaking of two different seasons in our walk with the Lord. The first comes when *"the violent take it by force,"* and the next as we *"receive the kingdom of God as a little child"* (Matt. 11:12; Mark 10:15). They couldn't be more different. There is the violence of faith, and then there is the power of rest. These two processes do not work simultaneously. They are two distinct seasons for two different purposes. And while they deserve more attention than I can give in this chapter, I will simply say that these two processes serve two different purposes in our progress and development.

When it is time for the violent acts of faith, it is because God desires for us to learn about our authority. Nothing else works during this time. Authority is exercised through faith in His Word, revealing what Jesus accomplished for us at Calvary. In the absence of our use of authority, little is accomplished. This is where the aforementioned hunger and pursuit come into play.

But when it's time to receive as a little child, there's an obvious change in seasons. While the hunger for more is still present, the pathway for breakthrough is surprisingly different. For in this context, He longs for us to learn about our identity. This is best seen in the posture of rest. We can fight for advancement in Kingdom experience, but we can never fight for identity. It is a contradiction in terms. We must *rest* into our identity. Some things only come through pursuit, others by "being."

WELL DONE, GOOD AND FAITHFUL GENERATION

Imagine a generation that properly received the full inheritance of the previous generation. In other words, their insights, their experiences, and their places of authority have all been faithfully embraced for the glory of God. They use it correctly and build upon it throughout their lifetime, leaving it for the next generation with the intended increase. Now imagine that process unbroken throughout Church history.

What would the Church look like today if we inherited the continuous momentum created by the faithful generations that have gone before us? Just the result of 2,000 years of Church history is unimaginable. Add to that the complete history of God's dealings with humankind from Genesis 1 to the present. All of that, and more, has been God's intention. And while we can't turn back the clock and redo thousands of years of neglect, we can take hold of the day that God has given to us. We can be faithful to discover what we have access to and train a generation to be able to manage it well. Living for a generation we will never see is central to this approach in our walk with Christ.

We are able to honor the spiritual giants of the past and access their anointings through such honor. It is not for the purpose of getting a title. It is so we can complete the commission our God and King gave to us. We need the breakthroughs of the past to position us for the breakthroughs of tomorrow.

FAREWELL BLESSING

My father died in January of 2004. It was a premature death, a tragic loss for our family. He truly was the father of a family, a tribe—a movement. His ability to bring strength and comfort in difficult times was legendary. I still have people who talk to me about the time he visited them in the hospital while they were sick. The comfort they felt was tangible. He was also my greatest encouragement and sacrificed greatly to make sure I was doing well.

We still live under the influence of the standards he set for a lifestyle of worship. It is the absolute priority of my life and now that of our church family. I have him to thank for that, too. Near the end of his six-month bout with pancreatic cancer, he laid his hands on each family member and prayed and declared the blessing of God in specific ways. It was a bittersweet moment. It was sweet because it was real, and he had something to give: an inheritance. It was bitter for rather obvious reasons. This blessing was patterned after the great patriarchs of Scripture.

There were 20 plus family members gathered together for several days leading up to his death—his home going. In the moments following his final breath, we circled his bed. I challenged the family with the need to receive his mantle and take it where he didn't have time to go. It would require a tribe to complete what he started. We prayed with each other, wept, and said yes.

In closing, I want to include a letter that I wrote to my dad, M. Earl Johnson, on a Father's Day, several years before his death. Inheritance is power.

Dad,

Because of you I started out as a good husband and father. I began "the race" with more than some finish with. That wasn't my doing. It was yours. Thanks.

Because of you (and mom) I grew up with the attitude that I could accomplish anything I really wanted to. That attitude wasn't the result of me trying to be positive. It was just there. Thanks. You gave it to me.

Because of you I stay encouraged. I watched you handle opposition graciously. You became the winner inside first, then the victor on the outside too. You have always encouraged me—never critical. My courage is strong...compared to many. But there again, that wasn't my doing. It was yours. Thanks. A million times...THANKS!

I love you,

Bill

ABOUT ERIC JOHNSON

Eric, along with his wife Candace serve on the Senior Leadership Team for Bethel Church in Redding, CA. He is a 6th generation minister and an author. Eric and Candace have a passion to see transformation take place in the lives of people, cities and nations. They have two beautiful daughters that make them extremely proud parents.

Eric Johnson
933 College View Dr.
Redding, CA 96003
www.ibethel.org
www.ericjohnsonministries.com

ABOUT BILL JOHNSON

Bill Johnson is a fifth-generation pastor with a rich heritage in the Holy Spirit. Bill and his wife, Beni, serve a growing number of churches through a leadership network that crosses denominational lines and builds relationships. The Johnsons are the senior pastors of Bethel Church in Redding, California. All three of their children and spouses are involved in full-time ministry. They have nine wonderful grandchildren

Bill Johnson
Bethel Church
933 College View Drive
Redding, CA 96003
www.BJM.org
www.iBethel.org